THE SECRETS OF
ITALY

Publisher and Creative Director: Nick Wells
Project Editor: Chelsea Edwards
Art Director: Mike Spender
Layout Design: Jane Ashley
Digital Design and Production: Chris Herbert
Copy Editor: Anna Groves
Proofreader: Helen Tovey
Indexer: Helen Snaith

Special thanks to: Sara Robson, Digby Smith and Cat Taylor

12 14 13 11

3 5 7 9 10 8 6 4 2

This edition first published 2010 by
FLAME TREE PUBLISHING
Crabtree Hall, Crabtree Lane
Fulham, London
SW6 6TY

www.flametreepublishing.com

Flame Tree Publishing is part of The Foundry Creative Media Co. Ltd

© 2010 The Foundry Creative Media Co. Ltd

ISBN 978-1-84786-956-2
Special ISBN 978-0-68101-756-6

Acknowledgments

Gordon Kerr (author) was born and brought up in the Scottish new town of East Kilbride. After graduating from Glasgow University, he lived in France before working in the wine trade in London for 18 years. He then worked in bookselling and publishing before becoming a full-time writer. He has written more than 30 books in a variety of non-fiction genres – wine, history, biography, humour, art, poetry and travel. He has a wife and two children and lives in Hampshire and South-west France.

Images are courtesy of Alamy and © the following photographers: AEP 148; Arco Images GmbH 192; Arcomano, Vito 168; CuboImages srl 16, 64, 96, 102, 142, 171; Dan Saunders Photography 138; Danton, Mike 42; David Noton Photography 92, 94–95; Danita Delimont 186; Forsberg, Peter 145; Fotomaton 178; Gerald, Eddie 127; Gio Spazz 2 35; imagebroker 30–31; ISIDORO RUIZ/IRUIZIMAGES.COM 11, 196–97; Jon Arnold Images Ltd 44–45; Joseph, Maurice 103; JOSEPH, NORMA 82–83, 105; Lebrecht Music and Arts Photo Library 76; luthy, yannick 93; Mackie, Tom 7, 34; MARKA 8, 88, 124–25, 139; Paul Thompson Images 54; Picture Contact 20–21; PjrTravel 97, 110–11; Pontino 23; shots from the hip 33; Stephen Saks Photography 155; Stock Italia 28; The Art Archive 101, 108; Travel Division Images 120; Welsh, Ken 84; www.vittorebuzzi.it 48. **Images are courtesy of Getty and © the following photographers:** Dallas Stribley/Lonely Planet Images 5, 193; David Noton/Stone 10, 15; DEA/G. Cozzi/De Agostini 188; DEA/M. Borchi/De Agostini. **Images are courtesy of Hugh Palmer** 4, 6, 56, 57, 87. **Images are courtesy of Photolibrary and © the following photographers:** Atlantide SN. C. 73; Bella, Michele 61; Bibikow, Walter 91; Bowman, Charles 180; Buss, Wojtek 43; Buttarelli, Eddy 75; Capone, Antonio 141; Cigolini, Gianalberto 37, 68; DEA/A. Dagli Orti 152; DEA/G. Cozzi 187; DEA/S. Vannini 5, 170; Galperti, Paroli 52–53; Giannotti, Alfio 140, 165; JTB Photo 66, 154; Kutter, Raimund 4, 89; Lombardo, Elio 112; Mackie, Tom 136; Masci, Giuseppe 166–67; Meneghetti, Federico 9, 162; Mesturini, Giorgio 163; René, Mattes 122; Sala, Riccardo 63; Sciosia, Vittorio 29; Signorelli, Enzo 175; Tomasinelli, Francesco 144; Tomii, Yoshio 60; Valterza, Renato 24–25, 26; Vidler, Steve 7, 128. **Images are courtesy of Shutterstock and © the following photographers:** Abrignani, Antonio 179; AndiPu 50; audisio, silvano 18, 109; Baldini, Claudio 14; Bobic, Nebojsa 85; Bogicevic, Goran 126; c. 22; Chaikin, Alexander 4, 40; crazy82 194; david5962 118; Davide69 32; del Castillo, Ana 74; Eliasson, Freddy 133; Farnetti, Maurizio 107, 113; Ferlito, Alfio 150–51; fotoecho 55; Fuxa, Filip 3, 81; g_m 106; Giampiccolo, Angelo 131; Hagge, Bianka 51, 200; Käfer photo 176–77; kated 153; Kistryn, Malgorzata 195; Kniukšta, Arvydas 182; Koltyrina, Lia 116–17; kompasstudio 98; Laporta, Alessandro 67, 69; Lebedev, Danila 36; Liska, Ales 181; luciano82 189; luiginifosi.it 183, 184–85; Iuri 49; m.bonotto 41; Malandra, Giancarlo 137; Melnik, Vladimir 27; Merrett, Paul 80; Mi.Ti. 1, 160–61, 164; mirabile 169; Mortula, Luciano 90; mountainpix 70–71; Nantel, Andre 132; Nekrassov, Andrei 72; Nobor 104; nrg123 99; ollirg 149; olly 19; Onigiri studio 38–39; Pieraccini, Massimiliano 100; Plechaviciute, Asta 129; RJR 62; Roca 17; Silviu, Hisom 123; Tifonimages 146–47; Trofimov, Alexander A. 159; Tupungato 5, 130, 174; Udvang, Thor Jorgen 121; vale_t 190–91; Valeria73 158; Veras, Maria 156–57; vieloryb 77; wjarek 58–59, 86, 119.

Printed in China

THE SECRETS OF
ITALY

WRITTEN BY GORDON KERR

FLAME TREE
PUBLISHING

Contents

ROME

SOUTHERN ITALY

ISLANDS

Introduction

TANTALIZING AND TREACHEROUS, INFURIATING AND DELIGHTFUL, BEAUTIFUL AND DANGEROUS. ITALY, THE *BEL PAESE*, IS ALL OF THESE THINGS AND MORE – A VIVID PATCHWORK OF REGIONS THAT ARE MORE LIKE DIFFERENT STATES OF MIND. AND YET, DESPITE ALL THE FRUSTRATIONS, DESPITE THE ITALIANS' OCCASIONALLY BRUSQUE AND OFF-HAND TREATMENT OF VISITORS, WE ARE STILL DRAWN TO THEIR FASCINATING COUNTRY TO WATCH THEM GO ABOUT THEIR DAILY LIVES, WHETHER IMMACULATELY DRESSED ON THEIR WAY TO THE OFFICE, OR IN WORKING CLOTHES WITH SKINNY CIGARETTE PINNED TO THEIR LIPS ON BOARD THE DECK OF A FISHING BOAT, OR YOUNG AND SEXY, CLINGING TO THE BACK OF A SCOOTER AS IT CUTS THROUGH THE MURDEROUS TRAFFIC.

They are a people of extremes, of high emotion and deep passion. It can be seen everywhere you look, in their art, in their cinema, in their literature and in front of your eyes every day on the streets of their towns and villages. But if Italians are people of extremes, then so too is their country a land of extremes, from the mountainous north to the sun-bleached south, the dramatically rugged west to the touristic Adriatic east. High art contrasts with crass tourism, poverty sits alongside great prosperity, beauty keeps nervous company with dangerous criminality.

As with most of the countries that fascinate us and attract us like sirens, the land and the people of Italy cannot be separated. Without the Italian character, Italy would not be as it is. It would still be beautiful of course, but the loud and often brash, yet cultured and often subtle (those extremes again!) Italian nature puts a different stamp on it. There is an inescapable vivaciousness that colours everything they do. And yet, there is also the dilatory part of the Italian psyche, the part that will always put off till tomorrow what could almost certainly be done today. There is always another thick, dark espresso to be had, or another hand of cards to be slammed down on the table of a local café, or another football match to be watched.

Nonetheless, this contradictory race once built a colossal empire that became the centre of the ancient world. It did not happen without the help of other great peoples, though. The Greeks came to Italy from the eighth century BC, fleeing political oppression at home or just in search of new challenges and a better life. These early settlers planted the seeds of civilization in the southern part of the country. They built independent cities, farmed the land and entered into trade with the land of their birth across the Adriatic. They also spread their cultural influence within Italy, introducing new artistic and architectural styles. The Italians learned from them how to defend themselves, how to build walls around their towns, and how to wage war.

The other great people to come to Italy were the Etruscans, who settled on the west coast around the areas of modern-day Tuscany and Lazio. The Etruscans provided a further civilizing influence on the locals and introduced them to new crafts, especially metal-working. Twelve independent Etruscan cities were founded and, like the earlier settlers to the south, their citizens traded with Greece.

One of their trading posts on the way to Greece was a small Latin village that began to flourish under their influence. Large buildings began to appear and the village became a town and then a thriving city. It was called Rome.

The Etruscans were overthrown in Rome in 509 BC and over the course of the next two centuries much of the southern part of the Italian peninsula was conquered. By 241 BC the Romans had thrown the Carthaginians out of Sicily and had taken Cisalpine Gaul. The onward march of the Roman Empire was relentless and a few hundred years later its territories were vast and barely manageable.

All the while, the incredible wealth generated by the empire enabled the construction of huge monuments to the power of the state, many of which remain today, giving us an idea of not only the ingenuity and engineering prowess of the Romans but also their huge ambition and unassailable pride.

The new religion of Christianity started as a small and insignificant movement, based in Rome where St Peter had

preached after the death of Christ and where the leader of the Catholic Church – not at that time known as the pope – would be based for the next two millennia, apart from the period of the Avignon papacy from 1308 to 1378. In AD 324 Emperor Constantine confirmed Christianity as the religion of the empire and Rome has been the centre of much of the Christian world since.

The fall of Rome in AD 410 led to centuries of obscurity for the people of the lands that would later make up Italy. Gradually, however, as the Middle Ages dawned, people once again began to organize themselves and great cathedrals began to be built across Europe. The Lombards who had invaded from the north introduced new forms of government and the papacy increased in power and prestige. The Holy Roman Empire brought the vast territories ruled by the Frankish king, Charlemagne (AD 742–814),

under the auspices of the church and, although there would always be tension between pope and emperor, it remained in place until Napoleon arrived on the scene in the early nineteenth century.

Italy, like many other parts of Europe, was victim to shifts in population and invaders. Normans, Saracens and Spaniards vied for power in the south, leaving their influence on towns and villages. Meanwhile, the republics of Venice, Genoa, Pisa and others grew powerful on trade and finance, their wealth leading to the extraordinary cultural explosion of the Renaissance. The humanities were studied and lessons were learned from Classical models. It was the age of Leonardo da Vinci (1452–1519), Raphael (1483–1520) and Michelangelo Buonarroti (1475–1564), an age of extraordinary artistic, literary, scientific and architectural achievement, many instances of which can be found in these pages, from Duke Frederico da Montefeltro's (1422–82) splendid Renaissance Palazzo Ducale in Urbino to Michelangelo's awe-inspiring Sistine Chapel ceiling. It was also the age of powerful and often despotic families such as the Sforzas, the Gonzagas, the Medicis and the Viscontis, the dynasties that ruled the city-states at this time.

For three centuries after the French defeated the Italians at Fornova in 1495, any hope of a unified Italian nation seemed hopeless. The nations of Europe vied for control, in a struggle eventually won by the Spanish, whose King Charles I (1500–58) was crowned Holy Roman Emperor in 1530. Later Italy laboured under Austrian rule and Napoleon Bonaparte (1769–1821) conquered much of the country in 1800, unifying it for a brief spell until the 1815 Congress of Vienna split it into its political divisions. The seeds were sown, however, and Italian patriots were given new heart.

In 1870, the uprisings of the *Risorgimento* finally unified Italy, making it at last a single political entity.

It is this history that has helped to create many of the wonders of Italy, the secret and not-so-secret places that draw millions of visitors each year. Although what remains of Roman times is mostly in ruins, one can with a little imagination gauge the scale of what they created. Of course, the Pantheon in Rome does still exist intact and its beauty and the perfection of its proportions speak highly of the skill and imagination of a people who seem to have been equally good at creating beauty as they were at perpetrating brutality.

In the Renaissance it was the unimaginable wealth and power of a number of individuals that enabled great artists to work under generous patronage to create their masterpieces. Pope Julius II (1443–1513) was one such and during his reign Italian High Renaissance architect Donato Bramante (1444–1515) fulfilled his greatest commission, the design of St Peter's Basilica in Rome.

Other patrons, of course, are less well known. Pier Francesco Orsini's (1523–83) bizarre Parco dei Mostri, designed by architect Pirro Ligorio (c. 1510–1583), is a sixteenth-century version of something that might easily have been conceived by Salvador Dalí (1904–89).

Some were not even Italian. Scottish botanist, Francis Neville Reid saved the beautiful Villa Rufolo Garden in Ravello from weeds in the mid-1800s, thus preserving a magnificent building and garden mentioned by Giovanni Boccaccio (1313–1375) in the *Decameron* for future generations to visit and enjoy.

Although unified now for more than a century, there are many who have difficulty in believing that Italy actually is one country, even among its own people. The people in the north accuse southerners of being lazy and benefiting from government handouts, and the southerners consider northerners to be arrogant and obsessed with money. And no one likes the Romans.

Geographically, it is a country of disparate yet always very beautiful elements. Indicative of the country's turbulent past, are the towns of Cortaccia in the Alto-Adige in the mountainous north-east of Italy and Alghero on the west coast of the island of Sardinia. Cortaccia's principal language is not Italian, but German. In fact, like many of the towns and villages of that area, it goes by a Germanic name – Kurtatsch – as well as an Italian one. Alghero, meanwhile, is often known as 'Little Barcelona' due to the prevailing Catalan influence in the town, in its architecture

Adige region winter sports rule supreme. It is these regions that dazzle the lover of wilderness, of sweeping vistas and breathtaking scenery. National parks such as the Parco Nazionale del Gran Paradiso offer wildlife, flowers and fauna and opportunities to enjoy vast unspoilt areas of great beauty. Close to the French border the valleys and peaks of the Val d'Aosta offer more skiing at resorts such as Courmayeur, and to the south Piedmont's mountains soften into wooded hills that conceal valuable truffles and produce fabulously delicious wines. The mountains of Lombardy also conceal treasures such as still lakes and sleepy towns and villages seemingly awed by the inestimable beauty that surrounds them.

The Apennines stretch down the spine of Italy, splitting the country in two. The rugged countryside of Campania in southern Italy smoulders with volcanoes such as Mount Etna, Mount Vesuvius and the volcanic island chain of the Aeolian Islands in the Tyrrhenian Sea just off the coast of Sicily. They belch smoke and lava and it is little wonder that the ancients dressed them up in myth and legend, usually as the gates to hell, or the forge of the fire god.

and even in its language. Some of its inhabitants speak a version of Catalan that has evolved little over the centuries since the northern Spanish ruled the area, and it is said that the linguistic equivalent would be someone speaking English today in the language of Chaucer's *Canterbury Tales*.

Mountains have always played a large part in the story of Italy. In times past the great city powers sprang up at strategic points from which trade routes could be controlled. The mountains also served as barriers to invasion and conquest. The country is punctuated by high, jagged peaks, especially in the Dolomites, which join with the Alps to form the country's northern frontier. Monte Bianco, or Mont Blanc, is the tallest peak at almost 5,000 metres (16,400 feet). Around it and across to Italy's Trentino-Alto

Italy's coastlines are also richly contrasting. The gorgeous, tiny fishing villages, such as Camogli on the Italian Riviera, the Ligurian coast with lush mountains rising behind, could not be more different to the sun-baked resorts of Sardinia, with their crystal-clear blue waters, bleached boulders and expensive marinas where luxury yachts line up at the quayside, their owners spending small fortunes in the restaurants and bars of former fishing villages such as Porto Cervo.

The beaches are superb throughout the country. Could there be a beach more dramatic or more beautiful than the one beneath the cliff on which stands the Calabrian town of Tropea? Its buildings seem organic, appearing to have merged with the cliffs on which they have been built. *La Spiaggia della Pelosa* (the Pelosa Beach) near the still largely unspoilt town of Stintino is breathtakingly beautiful and wild. One can only hope that this area is allowed to retain its rugged beauty and does not fall victim to the scourge of high-rise hotels.

The Italian countryside is, of course, stunning and varied. It is made for hikers. However, walking in the towns and cities is an equally rewarding experience. Can there be a more astonishing sensation than that of walking into St Peter's Square and taking in the history of the place? One particularly horrific story demonstrates the brutality of some of the powerful men who at the same time were responsible for enabling great artists to produce work of sublime beauty. According to the diaries of Johannes Burchard (born *c.* 1450), a leading official of successive popes at the end of the fourteenth and beginning of the fifteenth centuries, dishevelled prisoners were dragged into the vast space of St Peter's Square, their wrists bound, and every exit was blocked and guarded. On a balcony high above stood the 70-year-old Pope Alexander VI (1431–1503), the former Rodrigo Borgia. Beside him was his illegitimate and corrupt 20-year-old daughter, Lucrezia (1480–1519). On another balcony not far from them stood Alexander's son, the ruthless psychopath, Cesare Borgia (1475–1507). A servant handed Cesare a rifle, which he aimed at the crowd of ragged and terrified men below. A shot rang out and one of them fell to the ground. A servant handed Cesare another weapon, which he again fired, dropping another unfortunate victim. Only when all the prisoners lay dead did Cesare turn and walk into the darkness behind, his sport over for the day. Horror amidst extraordinary beauty can sometimes provide a paradigm for much of Italian history.

Although much of Italy's great architecture was created to worship and magnify God, it was also built to show off, to have a church or palace better, bigger and more ornate than the one next door or the one in the next town. But we would be so much poorer for the absence of the Duomo in Milan or the Fontana di Nettuno in Bologna. Less well-known buildings – the 'secrets' that this book tries to share with you – such as the curvaceous Stella Maris Church in Sardinia, further demonstrate the Italian love of beauty and their religious passion.

Ultimately, there really is no country on earth that can match the variety of experiences that Italy has to offer; no place that ravishes the eyes, tugs at the heart and makes the blood rush to the head quite as much as this fascinating land.

North-West Italy

THE NORTH-WEST OF ITALY PROVIDES A VARIETY OF EXPERIENCES FOR THE VISITOR, WHETHER IT BE IN THE FOOTHILLS AND SPECTACULAR JAGGED PEAKS OF THE ALPS, IN THE PLAINS WHERE GREAT CITIES SUCH AS TURIN AND MILAN CAN BE FOUND, OR ALONG THE CRAGGY, UNDULATING SHORELINE OF THE MEDITERRANEAN.

Experience is shaped by geography in these disparate settings. The mountains roll down into stunningly tranquil lakes, whose shorelines are dotted with quiet towns where the pace of life is relentlessly slow, as though everyone has to stop to take in the view every five minutes. And why not? Unspoiled natural beauty is an increasingly rare thing these days and the north-west offers a great deal. Indeed it is a far cry from the bustle of the cities, with their vibrant piazzas, busy streets and towering monuments to the past that reach for the sky as though to prove the supremacy of man. The Ligurian coast is different once again. Isolated villages, forgotten by the rest of the world until relatively recently, often balance precariously on the sea's edge as though they are about to topple in.

Italy is a country replete with cultural heritage, but its north-west in particular possesses an embarrassment of historic riches. Some of the world's most exquisite buildings can be found here as well as some of the world's greatest art. A lifetime would not be sufficient to fully explore it all.

Castello di Fenis

AOSTA, AOSTA VALLEY

Owned by the once-powerful Challant family, viscounts of Aosta, from the fourteenth century until 1716, the magnificently restored Castello di Fenis's extraordinarily evocative medieval architecture conjures up romantic images of knights and of damsels in distress. A keep surrounds pentagonal walls, protecting an inner courtyard adorned with precious frescoes. On the ground floor can be found a dining hall, a kitchen and a tax collector's office, while a chapel, reception hall and the counts' private rooms occupy the first floor, providing a tantalizing taste of medieval life.

Parco Nazionale del Gran Paradiso

AOSTA, AOSTA VALLEY

Graced by lush meadows, unspoiled scenery and dramatic mountain landscapes, the breathtaking wilderness of Parco Nazionale del Gran Paradiso, located in the Graian Alps, is home to Gran Paradiso itself, the only mountain over 4,000 metres (13,000 feet) entirely within Italy. Declared a Royal Hunting Reserve in 1856 by future king of Italy, Victor Emmanuel (1820–78), in order to preserve the dwindling Alpine ibex population, it became Italy's first national park in 1922. A wealth of wildlife – ptarmigan, chamois, golden eagles, marmots and rare butterflies – helps to make the park a paradise for naturalists.

Porta Pretoria

AOSTA, AOSTA VALLEY

The delightful town of Aosta, with its architectural gems and grid of imposing squares modelled on a Roman plan, is encircled by stunning mountain scenery at a strategically important point in the Aosta Valley. The magnificent Porta Pretoria, one of the few pieces of Roman construction still entirely intact, is just one of a wealth of Roman remains to be found; arches, amphitheatres and public baths have also been uncovered. Unsurprisingly, this place of great historical significance is often described as the 'Rome of the Alps'.

Monte Bianco

COURMAYEUR, AOSTA VALLEY

Nestled in a beautiful corner of the Val Ferret, at the foot of Monte Bianco in the Graian Alps, the celebrated little Alpine ski resort of Courmayeur offers numerous ways for visitors to disport themselves in both summer and winter. Skiers can enjoy 24 modern and functional lifts, consisting of cable-cars, ski-lifts and chairlifts, while snow-making machines ensure that there is always snow on the area's 100 kilometres (62 miles) of ski runs. In summer, hikers can visit Europe's highest botanical garden or revel in dramatic scenery and glorious surroundings.

Wooden Door

SALUZZO, PIEDMONT

To walk the streets of the charming hillside town of Saluzzo is like stepping back in time. It is divided into an unspoiled old town – buildings with red, tiled roofs punctuated by the remains of thirteenth-century town walls – and a 'modern' town that is itself centuries old. Saluzzo is a former medieval stronghold, which remained independent until 1601 when the Savoys won it in a treaty with the French. One of its best-known sons, Italian writer Silvio Pellico (1788–1854), used his own blood for ink while imprisoned for being a member of the Carbonari.

View of the City and the Mole Antonelliana

TURIN, PIEDMONT

Begun in 1863, the Mole Antonelliana was completed 26 years later, a year after the death of its architect, Alessandro Antonelli (1798–1888), who had originally designed it as a synagogue. A daring and iconic building, standing 167 metres high (547 feet), it is the world's tallest brick structure and, as host to Italy's National Museum of Cinema, is also the tallest museum in the world. A panoramic elevator takes visitors to a balcony for a spectacular view of the surrounding city.

Palazzina di Caccia di Stupinigi

TURIN, PIEDMONT

Situated 10 kilometres (6 miles) south-west of Turin, the impressive Palazzina di Caccia di Stupinigi was designed as a royal hunting lodge in 1729 by architect Filippo Juvarra (1678–1736) for Vittorio Amedeo II of Savoy (1666–1732). Delightful *trompe l'oeil* paintings and frescoes depicting hunting scenes adorn the walls of the sumptuous interiors of its 17 galleries and 137 rooms, 40 of which are host to a fascinating museum of art and furniture. Walkers in the palazzina's extensive grounds are greeted with broad avenues, beautiful parkland and striking formal gardens.

Palazzo Madama

TURIN, PIEDMONT

The magnificent Palazzo Madama imposes itself upon Turin's Piazza Castello, the descendant of a medieval castle that contained remnants of the original city walls. It was later enlarged and re-modelled with a new façade designed by Filippo Juvarra under the supervision of the 'royal madams' from whom it takes its name – Christine Marie of France (1606–63), wife of Vittorio Amedeo I (1587–1637), Duke of Savoy, and Maria Giovanna Battista of Savoy-Nemours (1644–1724), second wife of Carlo Emanuele II (1634–75). It is home to Turin's Museo Civico d'Arte Antica.

Vineyard

ALBA, PIEDMONT

The gourmet's paradise of Alba is home to the famous Ferrero Rocher chocolates as well as the white truffle. This gastronomic treasure, experienced at its fullest intensity in this area, is sniffed out in the surrounding hillsides every autumn by eager truffle hounds and, when found, can be washed down with one of the area's many captivating wines. In Alba many beautiful old churches coexist alongside Roman remains and its fourteenth- and fifteenth-century towers are commemorated each October in the famous 'Joust of the Hundred Towers and the Donkey Palio'.

Sacra di San Michele

SUSA VALLEY, PIEDMONT

Legend has it that angels helped in the construction of the Sacra di San Michele. It would not be surprising, for this religious complex clings impossibly to the summit of a mountain that guards the entrance to the Susa Valley and overlooks the plains of Turin. Originally constructed in AD 983 as a Bendictine monastery on the site of three earlier small chapels, this spectacular monument to religious faith, featuring elements of Romanesque and Gothic architecture, is acknowledged by law as the 'symbolic monument of the Piedmont region'.

Sacro Monte di Domodossola

DOMODOSSOLA, PIEDMONT

In 1657 and with the help of the local population, two Cappucine friars, Gioacchino da Cassano and Andrea da Rho, began the construction of a sacred mount, dedicated to the Passion of Christ, on the Mattarella hill, a rocky promontory dominating the town of Domodossola and its environs. Work began on the construction of 15 chapels, which were not completed until the arrival of the abbot-philosopher Antonio Rosmini (1797–1855), founder of the religious community, the Rosminians. To this day the Rosminians are the custodians of the sanctuary and its many extraordinary treasures.

Piazza de Ferrari

GENOA, LIGURIA

Genoa is a city filled with numerous vibrant and popular piazzas. The main square, Piazza de Ferrari, situated between the old and the new city, is dedicated to the Duke of Galliera, Raffaele De Ferrari (1808–76), whose palace is nearby. Home to public buildings, banks and offices, there is much to enjoy, including the splendid architecture of the Palazzo Ducale, the Teatro Carlo Felice and the eighteenth-century Academy of Fine Arts. Galleries, shops, restaurants and cafés add to the feeling that you are in the beating heart of Genoa.

Cattedrale di San Lorenzo

GENOA, LIGURIA

The striking black and white striped Romanesque exterior of Genoa's cathedral represents just one of the variety of architectural styles that have been employed in its construction over the passing centuries. Its side chapels demonstrate the Baroque and delicate French Gothic is also much in evidence. The ornate chapel dedicated to St John the Baptist contains a thirteenth-century sarcophagus reputed to have at one time contained the saint's remains, while the Museo del Tesoro di San Lorenzo displays fascinating relics such as a glass dish said to have been used at the Last Supper.

Galleria degli Specchi in the Palazzo Reale

GENOA, LIGURIA

The splendidly ornate Royal Palace of Genoa with its delightful red and yellow exterior was built by the Balbi family between 1643 and 1655. Renovated by the Late Baroque architect Carlo Fontana (1634/8–1714), it became home to the royal family of Savoy in 1825. Its Rococco interiors with their frescoes, stucco work, luxurious furnishings and precious paintings and sculptures remain spectacularly intact, while its beautiful ballroom and lavish Hall of Mirrors simply take the breath away.

Casinò Municipale

SAN REMO, LIGURIA

The faded elegance of San Remo on the Mediterranean coast of western Liguria is belied by the swanky yachts that jostle for space in its harbour. Its 'perpetual spring' climate has persuaded many notable individuals to make it their home, including Alfred Nobel (1833–96), Pyotr Ilyovich Tchaikovsky (1840–93), Italo Calvino (1923–85) and Czar Nicholas II of Russia (1868–1918). The gleaming white palace of the Casinò Municipale, completed in 1906, provides the town's main focus, but it is now probably best known for the San Remo Music Festival, held every year since 1951.

Street Scene

CAMOGLI, LIGURIA

Azure seas, stately resorts with casinos and promenades sheltered by swaying palm trees ... the Italian Riviera is all of this, but occasionally you will stumble upon a hidden jewel such as the alluring small fishing village of Camogli, situated beneath Monte Portofino. The name can mean either 'houses close together' – rendered appropriate by the tall columns of closely packed pastel-coloured houses that line the village streets – or 'houses of wives' – a reference to the women who stayed home while their fishermen husbands went to sea.

Medieval Towers and Cattedrale di San Michele Arcangelo

ALBENGA, LIGURIA

Until the Middle Ages Albenga was an important port, but when the sea moved further out the town was stranded inland. These days it is noted for its Romanesque brick architecture, especially the three magnificent thirteenth-century brick towers erected in the vicinity of the Cattedrale di San Michele, built a century earlier. A repository for fabulous paintings and frescoes, the cathedral was restored to its medieval structure in the Seventies. Roman and medieval relics, such as a fourteenth-century house on Piazza Girolama Rossi, add to the historical wealth of this fascinating city.

Courtyard

MONTEROSSO, LIGURIA

Monterosso al Mare is one of the five villages on the Riviera di Levante's craggy coast that constitute the dramatically beautiful area of the Cinque Terre. The villages are linked by the ancient footpath, the *Sentiero Azurro* (Blue Path), which provides walkers with unsurpassable views. Monterosso, however, is the only one of the five to offer the pleasures of a sandy beach, and as a consequence is a popular summer haunt for tourists. Originally accessible only by boat, the Cinque Terre now enjoys the protection of the Italian national park system.

Le Grotte di Toirano

TOIRANO, LIGURIA

The Grotte di Toirano is a remarkable cave system located beneath the lovely medieval town of Toirano. Amongst more than 70 caves in the area is the Grotto della Basura, which contains relics of palaeolithic life from 100,000 years ago, including hand and foot prints of Neanderthal men, women and children, graves and amphorae dating from Roman times and a collection of ancient bear bones. The Grotta di Santa Lucia is punctuated by countless spectacular yellow and grey stalactites and stalagmites, formed over hundreds of thousands of years.

Duomo

MILAN, LOMBARDY

Milan's huge cathedral, begun in the fourteenth century, was finally completed in 1965 with the inauguration of the last gate. One of the world's greatest and most beautiful churches, possibly its most striking feature is its roof, decorated with a forest of delicate spires and numerous sculptures and gargoyles, all supported by flying buttresses. The façade presents the viewer with a variety of architectural styles, from Gothic to Renaissance and Neoclassical, and light splashes onto the interior's five wide naves and 40 massive pillars, through breathtakingly colourful stained-glass windows.

Teatro alla Scala

MILAN, LOMBARDY

Following the destruction by fire of the original Milan opera house in 1776, architect Giuseppe Piermarini (1734–1808) conceived his design for its replacement as a 'stunning musical instrument' with exceptional acoustics. His severely Neoclassical edifice was named La Scala after the church that had previously occupied the site. It has become the most celebrated of all opera houses, the venue for the premieres of operas by Giuseppe Verdi (1813–1901), Giacomo Puccini (1858–1924), Gaetano Donizetti (1797–1848) and Karlheinz Stockhausen (1928–2007) amongst others.

Galleria Vittorio Emanuele II

MILAN, LOMBARDY

They call it *il Salotto di Milano*, Milan's drawing room, an extraordinary four-storey shopping arcade between La Scala and the Duomo, that opened in 1877, not long after its architect, Giuseppe Mengoni (1829–77) fell to his death from scaffolding. The first Italian building to use glass and steel as an intrinsic part of the structure, it is a haven for those in search of stylish boutiques, bookshops and cafés. For the gastronomically minded there is Savini, which offers one of the city's finest dining experiences.

View from Villa Monastero

LAKE COMO, LOMBARDY

Just a short drive from the hustle and bustle of Milan lies the serene tranquillity of Lake Como, Europe's deepest lake and one of its most beautiful. The foothills of the Alps rise dramatically from the water's edge and spectacular views can be had as you eat lunch at a lakeside restaurant in one of the lovely towns that hug the shore, Bellagio, Varenna or Menaggio, to name just three. The former Cistercian monastery Villa Monastero at Varenna is just one of many sumptuous lakeside villas.

Violin Workshop

CREMONA, LOMBARDY

Cremona, a market town on the bank of the River Po, is defined by its role as the cradle of violin-making, the greatest of whose practitioners was Antonio Stradivari (1644–1737). His instruments, some of which can be viewed in the Museo Stradivariano, now sell for a king's ransom. Numerous workshops continue the tradition. It is also the birthplace of the composer Claudio Monteverdi (1567–1643), after whom the town's music college is named. Cremona's pink marble Romanesque Duomo boasts a fabulous façade and the tallest bell tower in Italy.

Rocca Scaligero

LAKE GARDA, LOMBARDY

The fairy-tale castle Rocca Scaligera, also known as Castello Sirmione, lords it over the entrance to the town of Sirmione in what was once a strategically important position. Built by the Scaligera family, rulers of Garda in the thirteenth century, it is said that on one occasion the great medieval Italian poet Dante Alighieri (1265–1321) was entertained there. The castle fell under the rule of the Venetian Republic in the fifteenth century before being given to Austria by Napoleon Bonaparte (1769–1821) in 1797, returning to local governance after his fall.

Palazzo Te

MANTUA, LOMBARDY

At one end of the city of Mantua with its wonderful squares and aristocratic architecture stands the Palazzo Te, the former summer palace of Duke Frederico Gonzaga II, Duke of Mantua (1500–40). Designed and built by Giulio Romano (c. 1499–1566), one of the initiators of the Mannerist style, it was also lavishly decorated by him and his pupils. The Sala dei Giganti, for example, is painted from floor to ceiling in fantastically effective *trompe l'oeil* with a depiction of the giants attempting to storm Olympus.

Vineyards

SERMERIO, LOMBARDY

The tiny hillside village of Sermerio 'floats between heaven and earth', as someone once said, amidst stunning scenic beauty high above the blue of Lake Garda. It is one of 18 *frazioni,* or fractions, into which the *commune* of Tremosine is divided. Seventeen of these hover in the hills above the lake, while Tremosine itself sits closer to the shoreline. Across the water stands the imposing Monte Baldo, best viewed in all its magnificence from terraces high above the lake, such as the Terrazzo del Brivido, 350 metres (1,150 feet) above Garda.

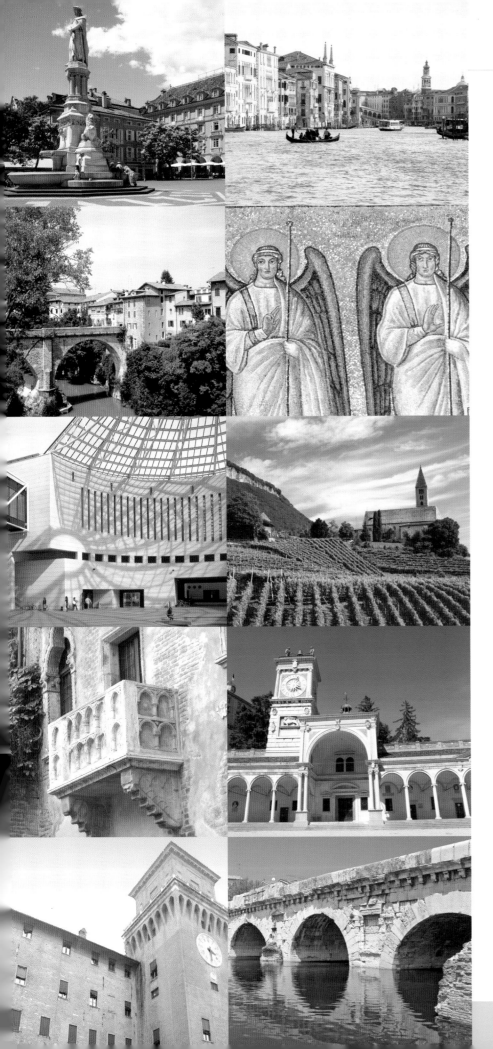

North-East Italy

The north-east of Italy offers the visitor a rich array of attractions, from the majestic vistas of the Parco Naturale Panevéggio to the startling, otherworldly beauty of Venice, from the grand villas that dot the rural hinterland to the castles and palaces built by the rich and powerful, and from the quiet antiquity of the Basilica di Sant'Apollinare Nuovo in Ravenna to the challenging modernity of the marvellous art to be found in the Museo d'Arte Moderna e Contemporanea di Trento e Rovereto.

The mountains of the region are home to ski resorts, where you could be fooled into thinking you were in Austria or Germany, while on the plains great cities such as Padua, Bologna and Verona vie with each other to offer the most spectacular architecture. There are historical surprises such as the town of Aquileia with its collection of important Roman remains, while lovers of horticulture can revel in the floral wonders of Padua's Orto Botanico.

The jewel in the region's already sparkling crown is, of course, Venice, a city unlike any other, where visitors stroll wide-eyed, taking in its vast range of architectural and historical pleasures. Every turn in a street or bend in a canal offers another delightful surprise.

You would be mistaken to believe that the north-east could never match the glamour of its neighbour to the west. If anything, there is an even greater variety of attractions for the visitor to savour.

MART

ROVERETO, TRENTINO-ALTO ADIGE

A vast cathedral to modern art, the impressive four-floor Museo d'Arte Moderna e Contemporanea, designed by the Swiss architect Mario Botta (b. 1943) and the Rovereto engineer Giuli Andreoli, was opened in 2002. The MART contains a staggering 15,000 paintings, drawings and sculptures, amongst which are works by Italian artists such as Giorgio Morandi (1890–1964), Giorgio di Chirico (1888–1978) and Carla Accardi. Contemporary international art is also represented by artists like Bruce Naumann (b. 1941), Richard Long (b. 1945) and Candida Höfer (b. 1944).

Pale di San Martino

PARCO NATURALE PANEVÉGGIO, TRENTINO-ALTO ADIGE

From rocky slopes to verdant Alpine pastures, from rushing streams to tranquil stretches of water, from miles of fir trees to mixed deciduous forests, and from icy glaciers to rich dark peat bogs, Parco Naturale Panevéggio offers a fascinating variety of natural environments. Situated in the eastern part of the province of Trentino, the park contains the magnificent Forest of Panevéggio, 2,700 acres of spruce fir, as well as vistas of the jagged peaks of the Pale di San Martino and to the west, the Lagorai mountain chain.

Houses with window boxes

VIPITENO, TRENTINO-ALTO ADIGE

Although the ski resort of Vipiteno is considered by many to be one of the most beautiful villages in Italy, its proximity to the Austrian border means that you would be excused for thinking that you were actually in Austria. Also known as Sterzing, its origins stretch back to the late tenth century and it mixes modern charm with medieval timelessness. Set amidst stunning natural scenery, the village is surrounded by mountains and hills clothed in lush meadows and woods, glaciers inexorably cutting their way through them.

Cortaccia

ADIGE VALLEY, TRENTINO-ALTO ADIGE

Cortaccia, a charming village dedicated to wine, sits at 226 metres (740 feet) above sea level on the enchanting Strada di Vino, or Wine Road, in the Alto Adige, where wine lovers can sample the local wines as they travel through the area. As they do, they will also be able to savour the dramatic backdrop of the Dolomites and admire the Tyrolean style of this predominantly German-speaking part of Italy with its beautiful timber balconies and overhanging roof eaves.

Trauttmansdorff Botanical Gardens

MERANO, TRENTINO-ALTO ADIGE

Located on a sun-kissed slope high above the sleepy spa town of Merano with its palm-shaded promenades, exclusive boutiques, upmarket hotels and fine restaurants, the gardens of Castello Trauttmansdorff are reputed to be the most beautiful in Italy. More than 100,000 different types of plants from all over the world are grown in four fascinating garden worlds – Forests of the World, the Sun Gardens, Landscapes of South Tyrol and the Water and Terraced Gardens. As though that were not enough, in every direction there is a breathtaking view to be enjoyed.

Piazza Walther

BOLZANO, TRENTINO-ALTO ADIGE

The city of Bolzano separates the Italian-speaking region of Trentino from the German-speaking Alto Adige or South Tyrol, but its old town still has the atmosphere of the Tyrol about it. The importance of wine to the region can be seen in carvings on the 'wine door' of its fifteenth-century Duomo, while its streets are lined with houses with intricately carved gables and balconies. The imposing Piazza Walther, over which the Duomo looms, is named after the thirteenth-century German troubadour, Walther von der Vogelweide (c. 1170–1230).

Basilica San Marco

VENICE, VENETO

Nothing prepares you for the Byzantine splendour of Basilico San Marco in which eastern and western architectural styles conspire to produce one of the world's most beautiful buildings. It is indeed a fitting monument to the remarkable history of Venice and a testament to the huge financial and political success it enjoyed as a republic from the late seventh century until its demise in 1797. The first St Mark's was constructed in AD 828, incorporating supposed relics of St Mark the Evangelist looted from Alexandria. The present basilica, situated just off the Grand Canal, was built in 1063.

Rio della Madoneta

VENICE, VENETO

Murky water laps against the walls of centuries-old buildings and the quietest whisper returns in a loud echo. Every now and then, people pass like ghosts across the elegant bridges that span the canals. The canals of Venice date back to the fifth century, when the people of the area began the construction of their city in a swampy lagoon as a way of keeping at bay the barbarians who were sweeping across Europe. This vista is on the approach to Campo San Polo, the spacious square that lends the *sestiere* (district) its name.

Canal Grande

VENICE, VENETO

It is one of the world's most remarkable journeys – a trip along the three kilometres (two miles) of the Grand Canal, past decaying pastel-coloured palaces built over 500 years in a pot pourri of architectural styles. There is no better way to see Venice's crumbling beauty than to take a *vaporetto* or waterbus along the canal. Amongst the countless breathtaking sights are the Rialto Bridge, the Ponte dei Scalzi and the Palazzo Capello Malipiero. No wonder it is described as 'the most beautiful street in the world'.

Palazzo Ducale

VENICE, VENETO

Perched on a network of loggias and arcades made from stunning white Istrian stone, the Palazzo Ducale, or Doge's Palace, a wonder in pink marble, is the grandest example of Venetian Gothic in the city. Founded in the ninth century, this airy masterpiece's present appearance can be dated to the fourteenth and early fifteenth centuries. Described by George Gordon Byron (1788–1824) as 'vast and sumptuous pile', it is filled with grandiose rooms, including the Sala di Maggior Consiglio, which accommodated the 480 members of the governing council.

Orto Botanico

PADUA, VENETO

The world's oldest botanical garden still in its original location was created in 1545 in the old university town of Padua on the property of the Benedictine monks of St Justine. Founded originally to cultivate medicinal plants, plants from all over the world were added, in particular from the lands conquered by the powerful Venetian Republic. It still preserves its original eye-catching layout – a circular central area representing the world and a ring of water representing the oceans encircling it – and to this day it functions as a centre for scientific research.

Glass showroom

MURANO, VENETO

Murano, like Venice itself, is a group of small islands linked by bridges. It was a commercial port as long ago as the seventh century, but has been the centre of the glassmaking industry since 1291, when the foundries were ordered to be moved from Venice because of the fire risk they presented. At one time, Murano glassmakers were the only ones in Europe who knew how to make glass mirrors, their craftsmanship so highly prized that they were prohibited, on pain of death, from leaving Venice.

Juliet's Balcony

VERONA, VENETO

The story of the tragic young lovers Romeo and Juliet is, of course, fiction, but that does not prevent tens of thousands of visitors from gazing up longingly at Juliet's balcony every year, wishing that Romeo really had serenaded his love from below. The sad truth is that the story was invented by Luigi da Porto of Vicenza in the 1520s, and that Casa di Giulietta, 27 Via Cappello, is actually a restored thirteenth-century inn. But when did we ever allow the truth to get in the way of a good story?

Bellringers at Castello di San Giusto

TRIESTE, FRIULI-VENEZIA GIULIA

There is an air of decadence about Trieste, a town that once dared to rival Venice in the Adriatic but now languishes in the backwaters of history. The narrow streets of its *città vecchia* (old town) hold many treasures, however, especially at San Giusto, which is, unusually, both a castle and a cathedral, constructed from buildings dating as far back as the sixth century. The basilica, created by merging two fifth-century churches, is adorned with superb thirteenth-century mosaics in the Venetian style.

Castello di Miramare

TRIESTE, FRIULI-VENEZIA GIULIA

The Habsburg Archduke Maximilian (1832–67) built the gleaming white Castello di Miramare as his summer residence on the banks of the Adriatic between 1856 and 1860. He would enjoy only a few summers there. In 1867 he was killed in Mexico, of which he had become emperor. Miramare is the definitive romantic castle, perched on a huge rock on the edge of the sea. It is still furnished as it was back then and its verdant gardens, with one pond for swans and another for lotus flowers, bear the tragic Maximilian's personal stamp.

View from Castello Nuovo

DUINO, FRIULI-VENEZIA GIULIA

Fourteen kilometres (8.6 miles) north-west along the coast from Trieste lies the pretty village of Duino, possessor of two castles. The eleventh-century Castello Vecchio today lies in ruins, but the fifteenth-century Castello Nuovo is the seat of the princes of Thurn and Taxis. Many notable people have enjoyed its hospitality over the centuries, including Archduke Franz Ferdinand (1863–1914), Franz Liszt (1811–86) and the poet Rainer Maria Rilke (1875–1926), who composed the first two of his famous Duino Elegies here.

Basilica mosaic floor
AQUILEIA, FRIULI-VENEZIA GIULIA

Strolling through the port of Aquileia, it is difficult to believe that it was once one of the largest and wealthiest cities in the early Roman Empire, where Emperor Augustus (63 BC–14 AD) once entertained Herod the Great (74–4 BC). Destroyed by Attila the Hun (406–453 AD) in the fifth century, it is now surrounded by ruins that hark back to better days. Luckily, parts of its early Christian basilica, a building that played an important role in the evangelizing of Europe, have survived, including its beautifully ornate floor mosaics.

Loggia di San Giovanni
UDINE, FRIULI-VENEZIA GIULIA

The historic capital of Friuli, Udine is a city with its own unique style. Opposite the Loggia del Lionello, the fifteenth-century city hall with its Venetian-style pink and white masonry and pointed arches and windows, stands the Renaissance structure of the Loggia di San Giovanni. Situated beneath a hill crowned by the town's castle with its impressive gallery of antique art, the loggia and its wonderful clock tower, modelled on the one in Venice's Piazza San Marco, dominate the town centre.

Ponte del Diavolo

CIVIDALE DEL FRIULI, FRIULI-VENEZIA GIULIA

The legend-rich fifteenth-century Devil's Bridge spans the dramatic ravine of the emerald-green Natisone River in the town of Cividale del Friuli. Retreating Italian troops destroyed the 22-metre-high (72 feet) bridge in 1917, but it was rebuilt after the armistice. Legend has it that at an earlier point in its long history the devil angrily threw the bridge into the flowing waters below. Cividale del Friuli is a charming town of cobbled streets with a rare example of an eighth-century church, the Tempietto Longobardo.

Duomo

GEMONA, FRIULI-VENEZIA GIULIA

Gemona del Friuli, a part of the Gemonese Mountain Community situated on the left bank of the River Tagliamento, is home to a wealth of extraordinary medieval architecture, not least of which are its Duomo and its massive bell tower, which date back to the fourteenth century but which came close to being destroyed in the catastrophic earthquake of 1976. The façade of the cathedral is adorned with sumptuous carvings and breathtaking rose windows, but it is the gargantuan seven-metre-tall (22 feet) statue of St Christopher that really catches the eye.

Mosaic in the Basilica di Sant'Apollinare Nuovo

RAVENNA, EMILIA-ROMAGNA

The beautiful and important sixth-century church of Sant'Apollinare Nuovo was built in eastern Ravenna as a palace chapel by Ostrogoth King Theodoric. Its walls are adorned with glittering mosaics created in the early sixth century and include 26 magnificent panels depicting the life of Christ. That they mostly exist in their original form is something of a miracle, one for which we should be eternally grateful. The basilica's exterior blends eastern and western styles in a way that was characteristic of its time.

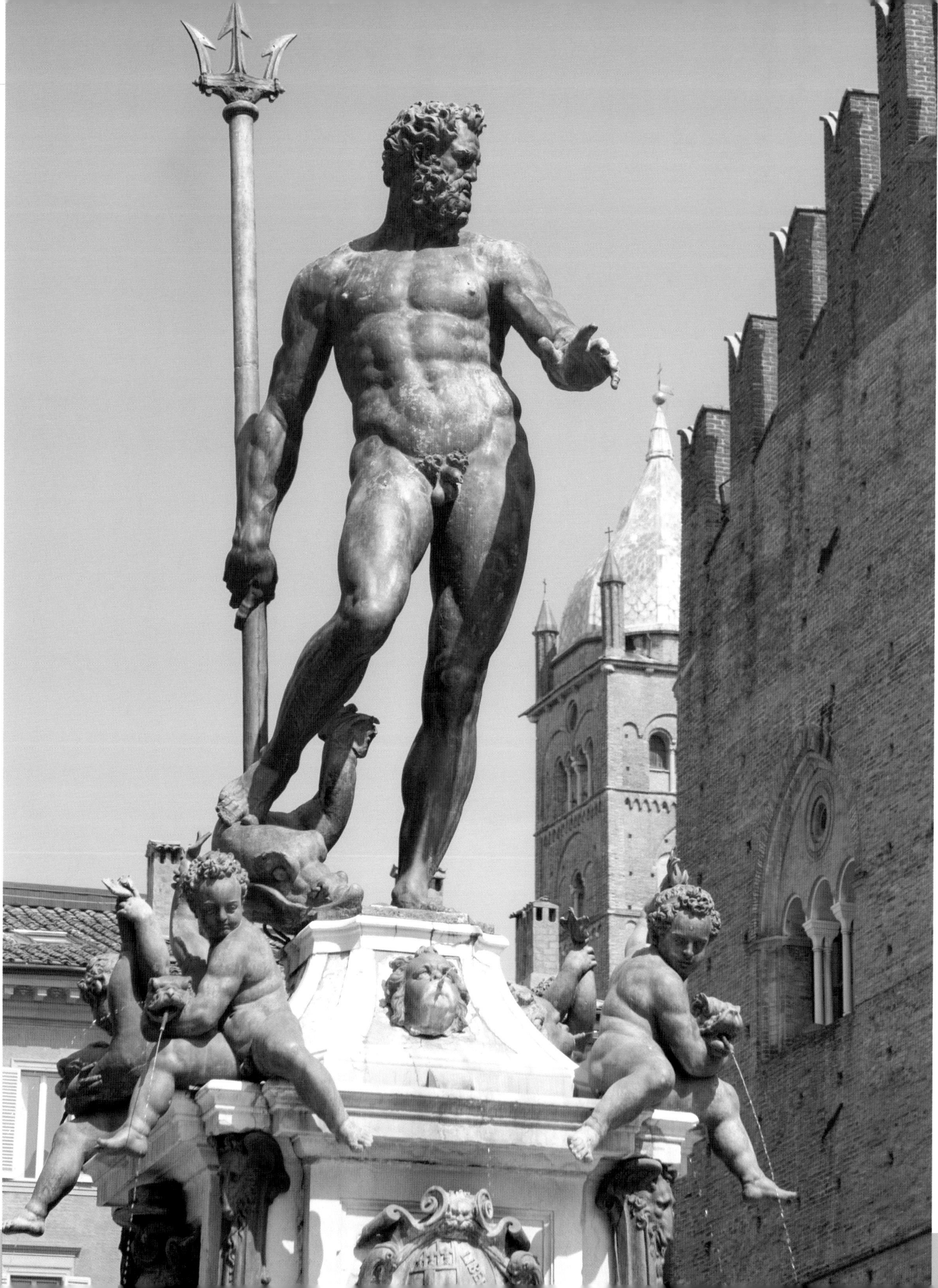

Fontana di Nettuno

BOLOGNA, EMILIA-ROMAGNA

An entire building was pulled down to make way for the Mannerist swirls of this dramatic civic monument. Commissioned by Cardinal Charles Borromeo (1538–84) to commemorate his uncle's election as Pope Pius IV (1499–1565), the base was designed by Palermo architect Tommaso Laureti (c. 1530–1602) in 1563, while the over-size bronze statue of the god Neptune on the top was made by Belgian sculptor Giambologna (1529–1608). Reaching his hand out to still the waters, the figure of Neptune has become an iconic symbol of the city of Bologna.

Piazza Maggiore

BOLOGNA, EMILIA-ROMAGNA

Medieval palazzos, built between 1200 and 1400, cluster around the Piazza Maggiore, which represents the true centre of the city of Bologna. Romanesque and Gothic architecture contrasts with the Mannerist Fontana di Nettuno, but the Church of San Pietro dominates the piazza, ambitiously designed to be even bigger than St Peter's in Rome but remaining sadly unfinished due to lack of funds. The Palazzo del Commune (town hall) with its beautiful bell tower stands on the right side and to the east lies the sturdy thirteenth-century Palazzo de Re Enzo.

Castello Estense

FERRARA, EMILIA-ROMAGNA

Built in the fourteenth century – and at the time a major feat of military engineering – the Castello Estense was home to the powerful Este family, a defence against the outside world. Some inhabitants of the Castello, angered by taxes and bad weather, ripped to pieces one of their officials in 1385. The Este court patronized artists such as Antonio Pisanello (c. 1395–1455), Giovanni Bellini (c. 1430–1516) and Andrea Mantegna (c. 1431–1506), but the building now functions as municipal offices, reminding us of its former magnificence in only a few of its rooms.

Delicatessen

PARMA, EMILIA-ROMAGNA

The prosperous town of Parma is synonymous with good food and good living. In fact, it is the good food that has made it so wealthy, its *prosciutto di Parma*, for instance, is savoured around the world. It also boasts some fine medieval buildings such as the Lombard-Romanesque cathedral and the vast Palazzo Pilotta, built for the Farnese family in the sixteenth century. Picturesque cobbled streets are punctuated by well-preserved monuments, while the city's delis entice the passer-by with their mouthwatering displays.

Central Italy

A LEANING TOWER, LAVISHLY ORNATE CHURCHES, EXQUISITELY PROPORTIONED PALACES, SPARKLING WHITE BEACHES AND IMPREGNABLE ROMANTIC CASTLES – TUSCANY, UMBRIA, LE MARCHE AND LAZIO HAVE MUCH TO OFFER. THEY ARE AREAS RICH WITH THE HISTORY OF MANY CENTURIES. THE TURBULENT AND OFTEN BRUTALLY VIOLENT YEARS OF THE GOTHIC AND RENAISSANCE ERAS ALSO COINCIDED WITH ARTISTIC, SCIENTIFIC AND TECHNICAL ACHIEVEMENT THAT HAS RARELY BEEN MATCHED DURING ANY OTHER TIME. THE EVIDENCE IS EVERYWHERE IN CENTRAL ITALY, FROM THE SOARING AMBITION OF FLORENCE'S DUOMO TO ARCHITECTURAL MASTERPIECES SUCH AS THE PALAZZO DUCALE IN URBINO.

Great artists used the patronage of the Church and wealthy and powerful individuals to leave their mark on the region and on history. In this way Giotto di Bondone (c. 1267–1337) was able to design the beautiful *campanile* (bell tower) at Florence's Duomo and create one of the great works of art – his magnificent fresco cycle at the Basilica di San Francesco at Assisi.

The unforgettable landscape and scenery of Central Italy is equally impressive as the man-made delights. The spectacular beaches of the North Adriatic coast contrast with the hilltop towns of Tuscany and Umbria, while castles perch at the top of high cliffs, villages cling to hillsides and ancient towns hang over the edges of seas and lakes. It is Italy at its most beautiful.

Galleria degli Uffizi

FLORENCE, TUSCANY

The Uffizi, here seen at night, is as strikingly beautiful as much of the art within its walls. Commissioned by Cosimo I de' Medici (1519–74) in 1560 as an office building for Florence's magistrates, it was designed by painter and architect, Georgio Vasari (1511–74) in a horseshoe shape, with the shortest wing bordering the River Arno, close to the Medici Palace and the Ponte Vecchio. One of the most famous of the world's galleries, the Uffizi is home to priceless work by many of the great masters of the Gothic and Renaissance periods.

Duomo

FLORENCE, TUSCANY

The distinctive octagonal Renaissance dome of Santa Maria del Fiore, known simply as the Duomo, is one of Italy's great sights, an enduring symbol of Florentine wealth and prestige. The first stone was laid in 1294 but the dome was only begun in 1420, the work of Filippo Brunelleschi (1377–1446). One of the world's largest brick-built domes, it stands six metres (19.6 feet) taller than the ornate campanile, designed by Gothic master Giotto. The Baptistry, meanwhile, is renowned for its three artistically significant sets of bronze doors.

Ponte Vecchio

FLORENCE, TUSCANY

The iconic Ponte Vecchio, spanning the River Arno at its narrowest point, was the only Florentine bridge to survive the Second World War, saved by specific order of Hitler. There has been a bridge on this location since Roman times, but its current design, by Taddeo Gaddi (c. 1300–66), dates from 1345. Shops line its span, while above them runs the Corridoio Vasari, an enclosed elevated passageway connecting the Palazzo Vecchio with the Palazzo Pitti that enabled Cosimo I de' Medici to move freely between his residence and the government palace.

Museo Nazionale del Bargello

FLORENCE, TUSCANY

The Bargello Museum, once a prison and place of execution, is now Florence's premier museum of sculpture, exhibiting work by some of Italy's greatest sculptors. Originally built in the mid-thirteenth century to house Florence's highest magistrate, this extraordinary edifice is the city's oldest public building. The museum is home to masterpieces by Michelangelo Buonarroti (1475–1564) and works such as Donato Donatello's (c. 1386–1466) stunning bronze, *David* – one of the most famous examples of Italian Renaissance sculpture – while Benvenuto Cellini (1500–71) and Lorenzo Ghiberti (1378–1455) are amongst other artists whose work is on view.

Campo dei Miracoli

PISA, TUSCANY

The Duomo di Santa Maria Assunta, the Torre di Pisa, the Battistero di San Giovanni and the Camposanto are all located in an area first described as the Campo dei Miracoli – 'the Field of Miracles' – by Italian poet, Gabriele d'Annunzio (1863–1938). In that one place the full splendour of medieval architecture can be viewed: the Pisan-Romanesque Duomo with its four-tiered façade, begun in 1064; the lengthy marble arcades of the Camposanto cemetery, begun in 1278; and that greatest miracle of all, the impossibly angled Leaning Tower of Pisa, begun in 1173.

Vineyard and Olive Grove

CHIANTI, TUSCANY

The unique undulating landscape of Chianti, with its verdant hills rich with vines and olive trees, charming stone villages, picturesque churches and striking Renaissance palazzos, is amongst the most beautiful and most photographed in the world. Extending roughly north to south over the provinces of Florence and Siena and west to east between Val d'Esta and the Valdarno, it is largely unspoilt and sparsely populated. Its delicious red wines such as Chianti Classico, Brunello di Montalcino and Vino Nobile di Montepulciano are prized the world over.

View from Monterchi

AREZZO, TUSCANY

The town of Monterchi sits like an island on a small hill in the centre of the Cerfone valley. The outcrop, known in Roman and Etruscan times as the Hill of Hercules, was home to a pagan cult that believed in the fertility properties of the local spring water. A town had been established there by the Middle Ages and by 1440 it was under Florentine control. Monterchi is today most famous for Piero della Francesco's beautiful painting, *Madonna del Parto* (the Madonna of the Childbirth).

Portoferraio

ELBA, TUSCANY

As someone once observed, Portoferraio is so well situated that it must have been chosen as capital of the island of Elba not by man but by nature. Located on a spur of rock, it spills down into the sea, its narrow streets behind its harbour leading up to its fortifications, dating from when the town was renamed Cosmopoli for Cosimo de' Medici who re-built the village in 1548 following its destruction by the Saracens. Amongst its notable sights is Villa Martino, residence of Napoleon Bonaparte (1769–1821) during his exile.

Duomo

MASSA MARITTIMA, TUSCANY

The town of Massa Marittima is a medieval jewel situated in the Maremma region of western Tuscany, an area still largely unknown to tourists but where authentic Tuscan culture can still be enjoyed. Founded, like many cities in Tuscany, by the Etruscans, amongst its notable sights is its magnificent thirteenth-century Duomo, dedicated to St Cerbonius, with its Romanesque and Gothic features, including a Romanesque font dating back to 1267. Amongst its artworks is the fourteenth-century *Madonna delle Grazie*, attributed to Gothic master Duccio di Buoninsegna (c. 1255–60–1318/9).

View towards Preci

VALNERINA, UMBRIA

Umbria is dotted with beautiful hill towns set in spectacular surroundings. The medieval fortified village of Preci is just one of them. Set high in the lush splendour of the hills of the province of Perugia, it is a stunning fortified settlement that was almost entirely destroyed by an earthquake in 1328. Apart from wonderful views it has a great deal to offer, including several notable churches, one with an impressive Gothic portal and another with a *pietà* (a depiction of the Virgin Mary cradling the dead Jesus) dating back to the fifteenth century.

Shop in Castiglione del Lago

PERUGIA, UMBRIA

The tranquil beauty and reed-lined shores of Lake Trasimeno, Italy's fourth-largest lake, is surrounded by low hills on the border between Tuscany and Umbria. On the lake's western shore stands Castiglione del Lago, occupying a fortified promontory that was once an island. Its *centro storico* boasts exceedingly well-preserved medieval walls and the Palazzo del Commune, which was built in Renaissance style by Ascanio della Corgna, a scion of the ruling family. On its walls are magnificent frescoes by Pescara-born artist Giovanni Pandolfi (1567–1636) and the Florentine artist Salvio Savini.

Oratorio di San Bernadino

PERUGIA, UMBRIA

On the right-hand side of Piazza San Francesco, next to the church dedicated to that saint, stands the lovely fifteenth-century Oratorio di San Bernardino, built on the spot where this Franciscan monk preached. The oratory now functions as a museum with numerous treasures to be viewed, including frescoes that are stunning examples of Sienese painting of the first quarter of the sixteenth century. The beautiful wood-panelled ceiling is decorated with cherubs' heads set against a blue background.

Ponte delle Torri

SPOLETO, UMBRIA

The 'Bridge of Towers' is aptly named. A high tower stands guard at each end of the magnificent fourteenth-century, 10-arcade bridge. Designed by Matteo Gattaponi (c. 1300–83), the structure stands 80 metres (262 feet) high, spanning a distance of 236 metres (258 yards). The magnificent panoramic view takes in the papal fortress of Rocca Albornoz and the lush Preapennine hills close to Spoleto, and inspired the eighteenth-century German writer and dramatist Wolfgang von Goethe (1749–1832) to dedicate a page of his *Viaggio in Italia* to it.

Duomo

ORVIETO, UMBRIA

Orvieto is situated on a plateau 300 metres (984 feet) above the vineyard-covered plain whose wine has helped make the town famous. It has also become well known for its magnificent Romanesque-Gothic Duomo, one of the great cathedrals of Italy. Begun in 1290, and inspired by the Miracle of Bolsena, when a consecrated Host (sacramental bread) is said to have bled real blood, it took 300 years to build. The exterior is decorated with horizontal bands of white travertine and bluish basalt, while the interior is rich with exquisite Gothic art.

San Leo Fortress

URBINO, MARCHE

Palazzo Ducale

URBINO, MARCHE

Perched on the edge of a sheer drop and overlooking the charming village from which it derives its name, the mighty, impregnable fortress of San Leo, built for the dukes of Montefeltro, is an astonishing sight. It featured in Dante Alighieri's (c. 1265–1321) *Divine Comedy* and was considered by none other than Machiavelli (1469–1527) to be the finest example of military architecture in Italy. In the eighteenth century, it became a papal prison but the state rooms and the towering Renaissance ramparts, designed by artist and military engineer Francesco di Giorgio Martini (1439–1502), remain wonderfully intact.

The Palazzo Ducale at Urbino is one of Italy's finest examples of Renaissance architecture and arguably the most beautiful Italian palazzo of its time. Built by the Duke of Urbino, Federico da Montefeltro (1422–82), its tranquil courtyard is surrounded by exquisitely proportioned rooms and spaces. His library, collection of paintings and the building's design have been described as 'the purest and most harmonious expressions of Quattrocento aesthetic ideals'. Priceless works by the great artists such as *The Flagellation* by Piero della Francesca (c. 1415–92) and *La Muta* by Raphael (1483–1520) adorn the walls.

Fontana del Calamo

ANCONA, MARCHE

Although heavy bombing during the Second World War sadly destroyed much of Ancona's old town, some real treasures remain, including the fifteenth-century Loggia dei Mercanti. At the summit of the Colle Guasco stands the town's most significant landmark, the beautiful twelfth-century cathedral of San Ciriaco, with its fabulous Byzantine art and a pagan temple in its crypt. The sixteenth-century Fontano del Calamo in Corso Mazzini cascades water from each of its row of 13 masked spouts that are said to be effigies of people who had been beheaded.

Pinacoteca Civica

JESI, MARCHE

The small Marche city of Jesi sits alluringly amidst the countryside in which the crisp white wine, Verdicchio, is produced. In its eighteenth-century Rococo masterpiece, the Palazzo Pianetti, is the Pinoteca e Museo Civica, which contains an extraordinary group of paintings created between 1512 and 1535 for the churches of San Francesco al Monte and San Floriano by the northern Italian painter Lorenzo Lotto (1480–1556). The central salon of the gallery is, meanwhile, an astonishing festival of fabulous Rococo decoration.

Monte Conero

CONERO RIVIERA, MARCHE

The coast of Le Marche is an endless chain of gleaming white, sun-splashed sandy beaches washed by the gentle waves of the Adriatic. To the south of Ancona the limestone peak of the 527-metre-high (1,729 feet) Monte Cornero soars above some of the most beautiful beaches on the Northern Adriatic coast. Three small resorts – Portonovo, Sirolo and Numana – struggle to cope with the huge number of people who jostle for space on their beaches in summer, but relief can always be found on Monte Conero's quieter flower-dusted slopes.

Festa di Quintana

ASCOLI PICENO, MARCHE

Every year, on the first Sunday in August, the town of Ascoli Picena stages its famous medieval parade. More than 1,400 townspeople dress in spectacular fifteenth-century costumes to recreate the Giostra del Saracino, a jousting contest between the town's six neighbourhoods. They parade down Piceno's charming main street to the steady beat of a drum, some on foot, others on horseback, before gathering at the jousting field where they cheer on their champions. The riders charge, lances thrust forward at cardboard effigies of Saracens and eventually someone wins but no one quite knows how!

Castello

GRADARA, MARCHE

The magical castle at Gradara stands 142 metres (466 feet) above sea level, against the stunning backdrop of San Marino, Rimini and Carpegna. Built between the eleventh and fifteenth centuries, it was the subject of conflict until being taken over by the powerful Sforza family. Its fame, however, is derived from its appearance in Dante's *Divine Comedy*, in the fifth canto of which the poet describes the tragic love affair between Francesca and Paolo, which he locates in the magnificent setting of the Castello at Gradara.

Villa Adriana

TIVOLI, LAZIO

Five kilometres (3.1 miles) west of the hill town of Tivoli are situated the picturesque ruins of Villa Adriana – Hadrian's Villa. This extraordinary complex of buildings was built between AD 118 and 134 by the Roman emperor Hadrian who, in an ambitious attempt to recreate some of the wonders he had seen in his travels, blended the architectural heritage of Greece, Egypt and Rome in order to create an 'ideal city'. The site is sprinkled with the ruins of theatres, libraries, bathhouses and formal gardens with fountains, statues and pools.

Tomba dei Leopardi

TARQUINIA, LAZIO

The Etruscans, who are believed to have migrated from around Troy, established their culture in Italy in prehistoric times. They seem to have been a people who enjoyed life and, indeed, the Romans and early Christians criticized them for being 'immoral'. Their enjoyment of life can be seen on the wall of the Tomb of Leopards in the necropolis of Tarquinia in Lazio, where a sumptuous banquet is taking place in the afterlife. Above the happy couples, the magnificent figures of two leopards, from whom the tomb takes its name, stand guard.

Parco dei Mostri

BOMARZO, LAZIO

The sixteenth-century theme park, the Parco dei Mostri, is the main attraction of the town of Bomarzo where, in 1552, the *condottiere* Pier Francesco Orsini (1528–88) commissioned the architect Pirro Ligorio (c. 1510–83) to create a unique garden following the death of his wife. Surreal, monstrous statues are distributed randomly throughout the garden in an attempt to astonish, not please, the viewer. Sadly neglected during the nineteenth and much of the twentieth centuries, the Parco dei Mostri was re-discovered in the 1970s, when a programme of restoration was begun.

Villa Lante Gardens

BAGNAIA, LAZIO

North-east of Viterbo stands the Villa Lante, named after the family who owned it for three centuries until 1933. Begun in the early sixteenth century, the villa was once the property of the Bishops of Viterbo, several of whom turned it into one of the country's finest Renaissance gardens. It is basically a formal Italian garden, arranged around the Fontana del Quadrato, a lavishly ornate structure surrounded by water on which there are stone boats. The garden rises in steps on which there are lively fountains and water features. Everywhere, however, there is perfection.

Alleyway

SPERLONGA, LAZIO

The whitewashed buildings, narrow streets and small squares of the old seaside resort of Sperlonga sit on a rocky outcrop about 100 kilomtres (60 miles) south of Rome. The Romans built villas on the coast and natural caves in the cliffs were made into places to dine. A little later, the town became the home of stranded English aristocrats and faded movie stars. Although much has changed, the sparkling white sand of the town's two magnificent beaches remains irresistible.

Door to Church of Santa Maria

VITERBO, LAZIO

The Second World War brought terrible destruction to the ancient port of Viterbo, but careful restoration has returned much of the town's grey-stone medieval heart to its former glory. Viterbo has had an illustrious past and in the thirteenth century was briefly the papal seat. Its wonderful buildings bear testimony to its former greatness, the old San Pellegrino quarter especially. The Romanesque Church of Santa Maria della Verità, outside the walls of the city, has wonderful fifteenth-century frescoes as well as richly ornate doors.

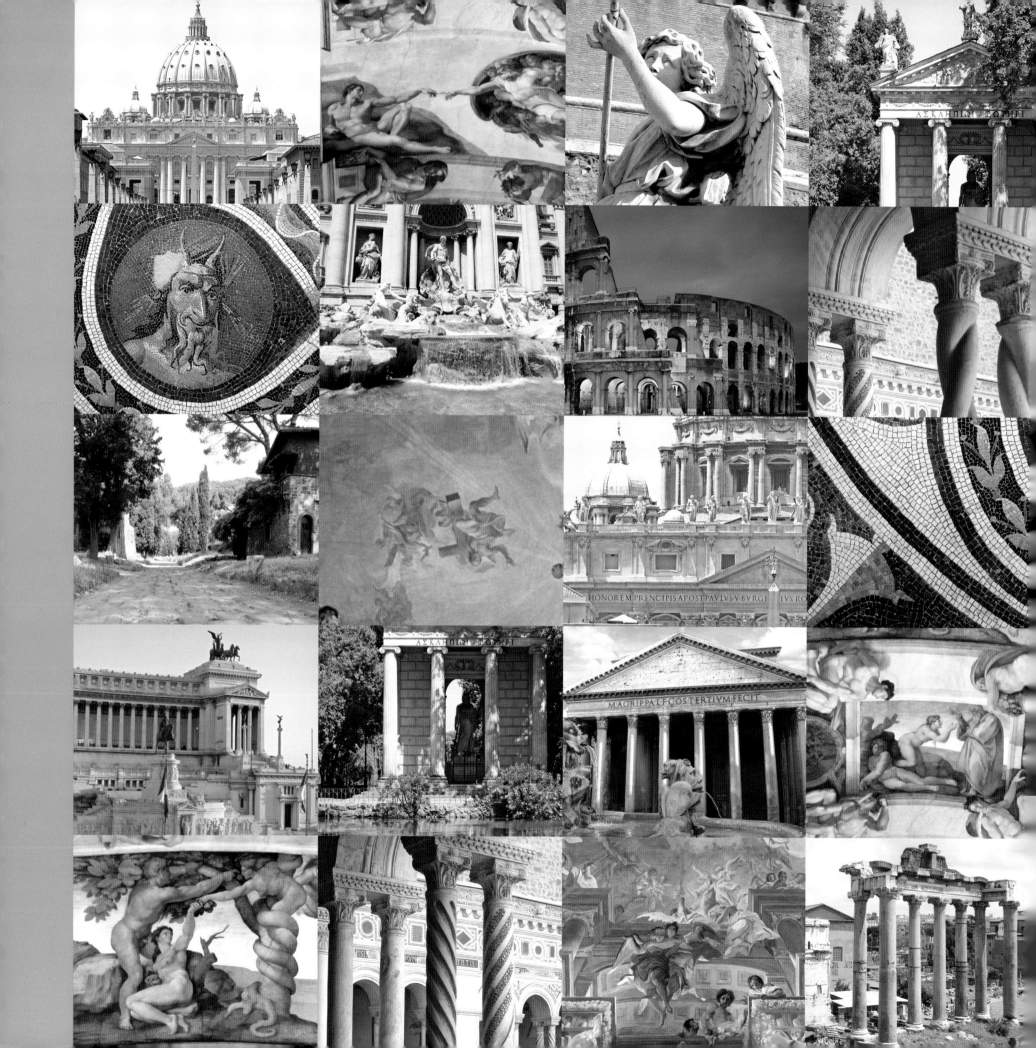

Rome

WHAT IS THERE TO SAY ABOUT ROME THAT HAS NOT ALREADY BEEN SAID THROUGH THE CENTURIES BY COUNTLESS POETS, WRITERS, PHILOSOPHERS AND TRAVELLERS? THIS ENDLESSLY FASCINATING CITY HAS BEEN THE CENTRE OF THE WORLD FOR A VERY LONG TIME, INITIALLY AS THE CENTRE OF ONE OF THE GREAT EMPIRES THAT RULED MUCH OF THE KNOWN WORLD, AND THEN AS THE FOCAL POINT OF ONE OF THE WORLD'S GREAT RELIGIONS.

All roads do, indeed, lead to Rome and people have been travelling them for a very long time. Nowadays, of course, we travel to the Eternal City to enjoy the countless historical, architectural and artistic treasures it has to offer. As we wander through the Forum Romanorum with its array of ancient ruins, we can only imagine the wonder that the visitor must have felt all those centuries ago when the structures were intact. Other marvels were later added to the Roman skyline, such as the Basilica of St Peter, a splendid example of Baroque style.

The power and wealth Rome enjoyed for such a long time has facilitated the creation of sublime works of art such as Michelangelo Buonarroti's (1475–1564) breathtaking Sistine Chapel ceiling and the many other priceless paintings, frescoes, mosaics and statues that allow this city to vie for the title of the world's greatest.

Basilica di San Pietro

VATICAN CITY

St Peter's Basilica, the epicentre of the Roman Catholic religion, was begun by Pope Julius II (1443–1513) in 1506 with Donato Bramante (1444–1514) as chief architect. In 1547 Michelangelo replaced Bramante, adding the magnificent dome and amending other elements of the plans. Dedicated by Pope Urban VIII (1568–1644) in 1626 St Peter's is an extraordinarily impressive building. The largest church in the world with the largest dome, its interior is decorated with the work of some of history's greatest artists, including Gian Lorenzo Bernini (1598–1680), Antonio Canova (1757–1822) and Michelangelo himself.

Ceiling of the Sistine Chapel

VATICAN CITY

The Sistine Chapel is one of the soaring achievements of humankind, a four-year labour of love by Michelangelo who was commissioned in 1508 by Pope Julius II. In stunning colour and striking detail, the artist tells the stories of the Creation of the World and the Fall of Man. Meanwhile, around these two main themes are subjects from the Old and New Testaments. Recent restoration work using computers, photography and spectrum technology has revealed even more vibrant colours beneath the layers of dirt and dusky varnish.

Statue beside the Castel Sant'Angelo

BORGO

The imposing cylindrical fortress of Sant'Angelo was built as a mausoleum for Emperor Hadrian (AD 76–138) on the right bank of the River Tiber. In the thirteenth century, however, it was acquired by the papacy and turned into a papal residence. Danger was never far away, however, and in 1277, Pope Nicholas III (1210/20–80) ordered the construction of an 800-metre-long (874 yards) fortified corridor known as the Passetto di Borgo, which could serve as an escape route for the pontiff should the castle be threatened from the outside.

Shop on the Via dei Coronari

PONTE

One of the most beautiful little shopping streets in Rome, Via dei Coronari derives its name from the sellers of rosaries (rosary beads used to be called crowns of beads), garlands and other religious artifacts, who used to congregate here to sell their wares to the pilgrims who flocked along the street, heading for St Peter's. The Middle Ages, the Renaissance and the Baroque coalesce in the lanes and squares but, although a medieval feel remains, the stalls of yesteryear have given way to shops selling expensive antiques and bric-a-brac.

Temple in the Gardens of Villa Borghese

CAMPO MARZO

North of the usually crowded Spanish Steps lies Rome's largest public park with its beautiful lake, fountains, temples and statues, created in 1605 when Cardinal Scipione Borghese (1576–1633) decided to turn a vineyard into a park. In 1903 the city of Rome obtained the park from the Borghese family and opened it to the public who can now enjoy its wide, shaded avenues, its tinkling fountains and its museums, including the *Museo e Galleria Borghese* housed in the beautiful Villa Borghese itself.

Café in the Piazza Navona

PARIONE

They call it 'Rome's living room' so popular is it with Romans enjoying their leisure time. Originally an open-air venue built by Emperor Domitian (AD 51–96), it was the principal market of Rome for 300 years. Now its three fountains, the Fontana di Nettuno, the Fontana del Moro and the most famous, the Fontana dei Quattro Fiumi, play in the summer sun as Romans parade or make their way to one of the many cafés and restaurants that entice the passer-by on the east side of the square.

The Pantheon

PIGNA

A temple has stood on the site of the Pantheon since 25 BC. The present building, the best-preserved ancient building in Rome, was probably rebuilt in AD 118 by the Emperor Hadrian, an elegant rebuttal to all who are sceptical about Roman architecture. The perfect proportions of this round temple are lit by its one source of light, the *occulus*, a large hole in the middle of the dome. Converted into a church in AD 609, it now houses the tombs of the famous Renaissance artist, Raphael (1483–1520), and several Italian kings.

Ceiling of the Rooms of St Ignatius

PIGNA

Angels, cherubs and beautiful youths appear to soar heavenwards through the extraordinary *trompe l'oeil* ceiling of this 1626 church, painted by Andrea Pozzo (1642–1709). The ceiling and, indeed, the entire church symbolize and honour the success of the priests of the Jesuit order founded by St Ignatius of Loyala (1491–1556), one of the leading figures of the Counter-Reformation. Its design is a soaring example of Baroque style, its glittering interior lavishly adorned by precious stones, beautiful marble and ornate gilt.

Fontana di Trevi

TREVI

The most beautiful fountain of the many that grace Rome's piazzas, the much-loved Trevi Fountain dominates the tight little Trevi Square in the capital's Quirinale district. Commissioned by Pope Clement XII (1652–1740) in 1732 and completed in 1762, it features Neptune riding a chariot in the shape of a shell, pulled by two seahorses. Meanwhile, statues to his left and right represent Abundance and Salubrity respectively. Turn your back and toss a coin over your shoulder into the Trevi Fountain and legend has it that one day you will return to Rome.

Mosaic in the Museo Nazionale Romano

CASTRO PRETORIO

The collection of Classical art that belongs to the Museo Nazionale Romano is so huge that it has to be housed in five venues – the Baths of Diocletian, the Crypta Balbi, the Aula Ottagona, the Palazzo Altemps and the Palazzo Massimo alle Terme. At the Palazzo Massimo are exhibits dating from the second century BC to the fourth century AD, the highlight of which is the marvellous collection of frescoes and floor mosaics from the villas of wealthy Romans, especially the Villa of Livia (58 BC–AD 29), wife of Emperor Augustus (63 BC–AD 14).

Colosseum

CELIO

There is a ruined beauty about the Colosseum. The largest building of its time, it was completed in AD 80, a year after the death of Emperor Vespasian (AD 9–79) who had commissioned it eight years earlier. It is immense, at 188 metres (616 feet) long and 156 high (511 feet), and 55,000 screaming spectators could be crammed in to gawp at the brutal gladiatorial combat staged here. An earthquake in AD 847 brought down the building's southern side, material from it being removed for the construction of later buildings, including St Peter's.

Cloisters of San Giovanni in Laterano

MONTI

Before the papacy re-located to Avignon in 1309, the Lateran Palace was the official residence of the pope. The adjacent church, San Giovanni in Laterano, still functions as the city's cathedral, where the pope officiates in his role as Bishop of Rome. Founded by Emperor Constantine in the fourth century AD, it retains its original basilica form, but was restored in 1646 by the Baroque Swiss-Italian architect Francesco Borromini (1599–1667). The cathedral's tranquil cloisters, built around 1220, are notable for their curious twisted columns and beautiful marble mosaics.

The Roman Forum

MONTI/CAMPITELLI

To the Romans, a forum was civic centre, but it also served as a shopping centre and a place of worship. Until the nineteenth century, the area that had once been Rome's hub was largely unexcavated, but since then a breathtaking array of temples, public buildings, shops and arches has been uncovered. The forum was first developed in the seventh century BC and expanded until it became the very heart of the Roman Empire. Today it is a maze of architectural treasures, each more astonishing than the last.

Vittorio Emanuele II Monument

CAMPITELLI

Every town and city in Italy honours the heroes who led the country to unification in the late nineteenth century. Their names grace streets and squares but the monument to the unified country's first king, Vittorio Emanuele II (1820–78), adjacent to the Roman Forum, is far from the most loved in Rome. Indeed, it rejoices in nicknames such as 'The Typewriter' and 'The False Teeth'. However, there is a very good reason to visit it. A glass-walled elevator climbs to the roof from which one of the best views of the city can be enjoyed.

Piazza del Campidoglio

CAMPITELLI

Michelangelo was responsible for the re-design of the Capitoline after Pope Paul III (1468–1549) was embarrassed by its muddy condition during a 1536 visit by Holy Roman Emperor Charles V (1500–58). The great artist proposed adding the Palazzo Nuovo in the shape of a trapezium, complete with Classical sculptures. Work began in 1546, but Michelangelo lived to see only the completion of the double flight of steps, the Cordonata, at the entrance to the Palazzo Senatorio. The piazza was finally completed in the seventeenth century, the design remaining largely faithful to Michelangelo's.

Via Appia Antica

LEADING TO THE CITY

The famous road, the Via Appia, along which St Paul was led to Rome as a prisoner, once linked the ancient capital to the ports of Taranto and Brindisi. Lined in places with crumbling family tombs, monuments and burial places, it is also said to be where Jesus met St Peter as he fled the capital – the aptly named Church of *Quo Vadis?* ('Where are you going?') marks the spot. Meanwhile, beneath the adjacent fields lie miles of catacombs. Near Rome, the road becomes part of a lovely nature and archaeological park where traffic is banned on Sundays.

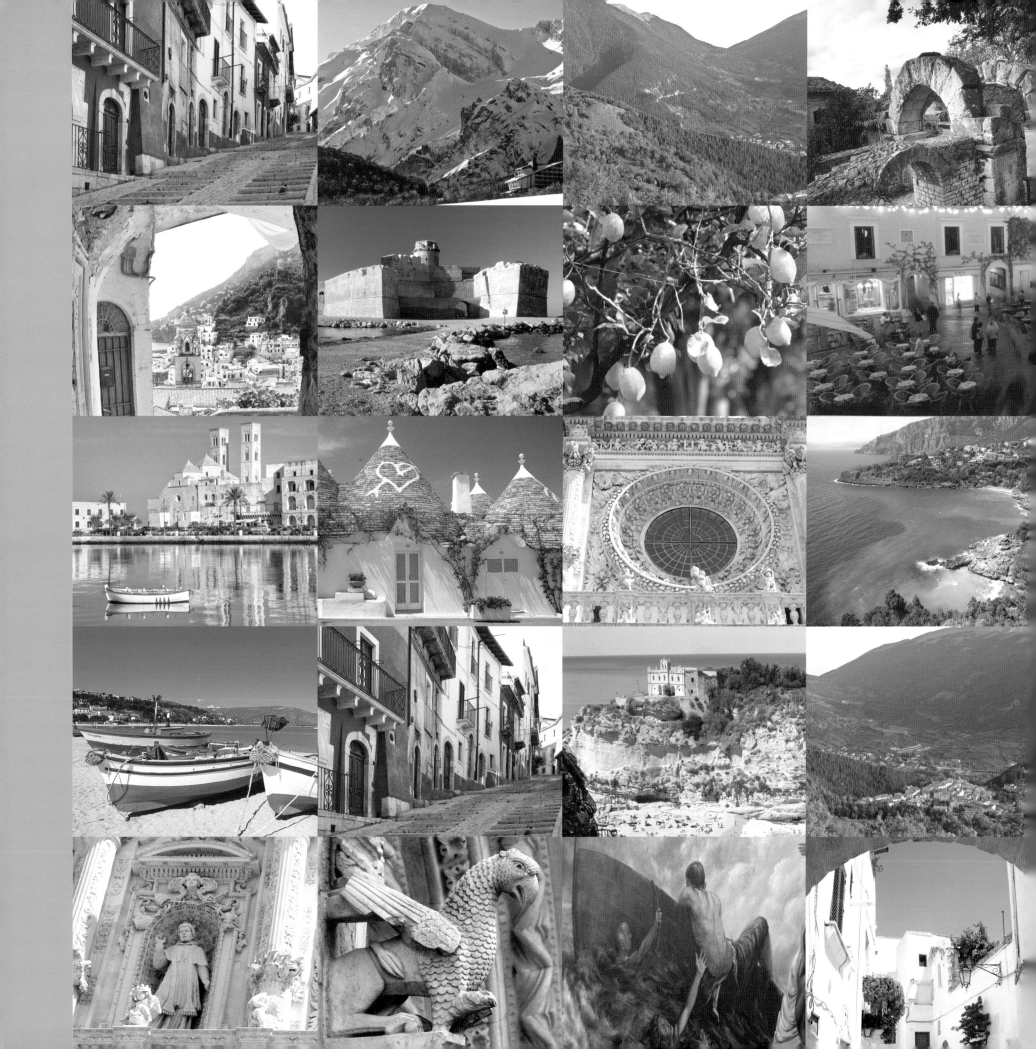

Southern Italy

SOUTHERN ITALY, A REGION OF MAGIC, MYSTERY AND DRAMA, MAY WELL BE ITALY AT ITS MOST DIVERSE. IT HAS EVERYTHING: CHAOTIC, NOISY CITIES WITH AN AIR OF DANGER; TRANQUIL NATIONAL PARKS WHERE RARE CREATURES ROAM; FADING HOLIDAY RESORTS WITH EXTRAORDINARY, GOLDEN BEACHES; AND ROMAN RUINS THAT ILLUMINATE THE LIVES OF FABULOUS ANCESTORS. IT ALSO HAS NAPLES, A PULSATING, CHAOTIC AND SOMETIMES THREATENING CITY THAT LUXURIATES IN ITS ROLE AS THE CAPITAL OF THE *MEZZOGIORNO*, UNDER THE SHADOW OF THE VOLCANO VESUVIUS.

The southern Italians are a passionate people, as can be seen in the religious celebrations that take place in this area. Festivals with ritual embedded in the deep past are played out in the crowded streets of small towns, passions overflowing, as well as wine glasses.

The south surprises and delights. The crumbling Baroque elegance of Lecce is startling, but not quite as startling as the other-worldly nature of the *trulli* of Alberobello – thatched, conical structures from which one would not be surprised to see hobbits emerge.

The past is ever-present in this region. The fascinating ruins of Saepinum and Baía remind us of life several millennia ago and the tragically beautiful ruins of Pompeii bring home the callous cruelty of nature amidst the stunning beauty of this ravishing part of Italy.

Stairway

L'AQUILA,
ABRUZZO

Rarely do horror and beauty mix as poignantly as in the lovely Abruzzo city of L'Aquila, cultural and historic centre of the region, but devastated by a powerful earthquake in 2009. Many died and large parts of the city, founded in the thirteenth century by Holy Roman Emperor Frederick II of Hohenstaufen (1194–1250), were destroyed. However, many of the town's buildings, which are laid out in the shape of the constellation of the eagle, giving the town its name, survived and for that we should be eternally grateful.

Gran Sasso

PARCO NAZIONALE DEL
GRAN SASSO, ABRUZZO

The spectacular jagged peak of the 2,912-metre (9554 feet) high Gran Sasso mountain is the centrepiece of the magnificent Parco Nazionale del Grand Sasso. One of the largest protected areas in Europe, the park is also one of Europe's most biologically diverse areas, with more than 2000 species of plants and vegetables, some of which are found only in this region. Rare animals such as the Abruzzo chamois can be seen as well as wolves, wild boars and magnificent golden eagles.

Piazza Garibaldi

SULMONA,
ABRUZZO

Named after the great hero of the Risorgimento, Piazza Garibaldi is one of the largest squares in Italy and in late July is host to an annual Palio. The square is also famous for the spectacular tradition of the *Madonna che Scappa* ('the Madonna that escapes'), staged every Easter. A statue of the Virgin Mary, covered in a black cloak, is carried shoulder-high from the church of San Filippo Neri. Amidst the noise of exploding firecrackers, the young men break into a run and her black cloak flies off when she 'recognizes' the statue of the resurrected Christ.

Civitella Alfedena

PARCO NAZIONALE
D'ABRUZZO, ABRUZZO

Just one paved road crosses the 150,000-acre wilderness of the Parco Nazionale d'Abruzzo, at the heart of which sits the pretty village of Civitella Alfadena on the slopes of Monte Sterpi d'Alto. Most of the park is carpeted with huge forests, which are home to a variety of endangered species such as the Apennine wolf, the Apennine lynx and the extremely rare Marsican bear of which few remain. A network of trails and paths criss-crosses the splendid isolation of this magnificent wild space.

Olive Groves

LORETO APRUTINO, ABRUZZO

Situated south-west of Pescara, amongst hills carpeted with the olive trees that are the mainstay of the local economy, the town of Loreto Aprutino grew up in the eleventh century around a Benedictine abbey and the castle that is now the imposing Palazzo Chiola. Around that time, the church and bell tower of San Pietro Apostolo that are also silhouetted against the blue of the southern sky were built. The importance of the town in medieval times is marked by the numerous works of art that adorn its fascinating medieval centre.

Fountain in the Borgo Antico

TÉRMOLI, MOLISE

Between Térmoli's busy beach and small harbour sits its attractive *borgo antico* (old town), whose entrance is guarded by the town's best-known landmark, a small castle built by Frederick II in 1247. In the fascinating old town beyond, a labyrinth of streets awaits, crowded with souvenir shops and medieval houses. Then, as the sun goes down, the inhabitants of Térmoli take to the streets to indulge in the southern Italian tradition of the *passeggiata*, a relaxed stroll, which is all about the being seen rather than the seeing.

Corpus Domini Sagra dei Misteri procession

CAMPOBASSO, MOLISE

The Festival of the Mysteries is one of the most important and evocative expressions of popular culture in the southern Italian region of Molise, taking place each year on the day of the Feast of Corpus Christi. Religious scenes are spectacularly depicted on platforms carried through the packed streets of the town of Campobasso. Children dressed as angels hang magically in mid-air and adults dressed as Old Testament prophets, demons and saints look down on the crowds below from their precarious positions.

Saepinum

NEAR SEPINO, MOLISE

Saepinum has simply crumbled back into the landscape over the centuries since it was abandoned around the fourth century AD. A small rural Roman town, it was initially important in the first couple of centuries AD, when it experienced something of an economic boom due to its position at the junction of two main roads. Now all that remains are the ruins of its fortified walls, its 25 round, defensive towers, thermal baths, a 3,000-seat theatre, the walls of shops and houses and the ghosts of its inhabitants.

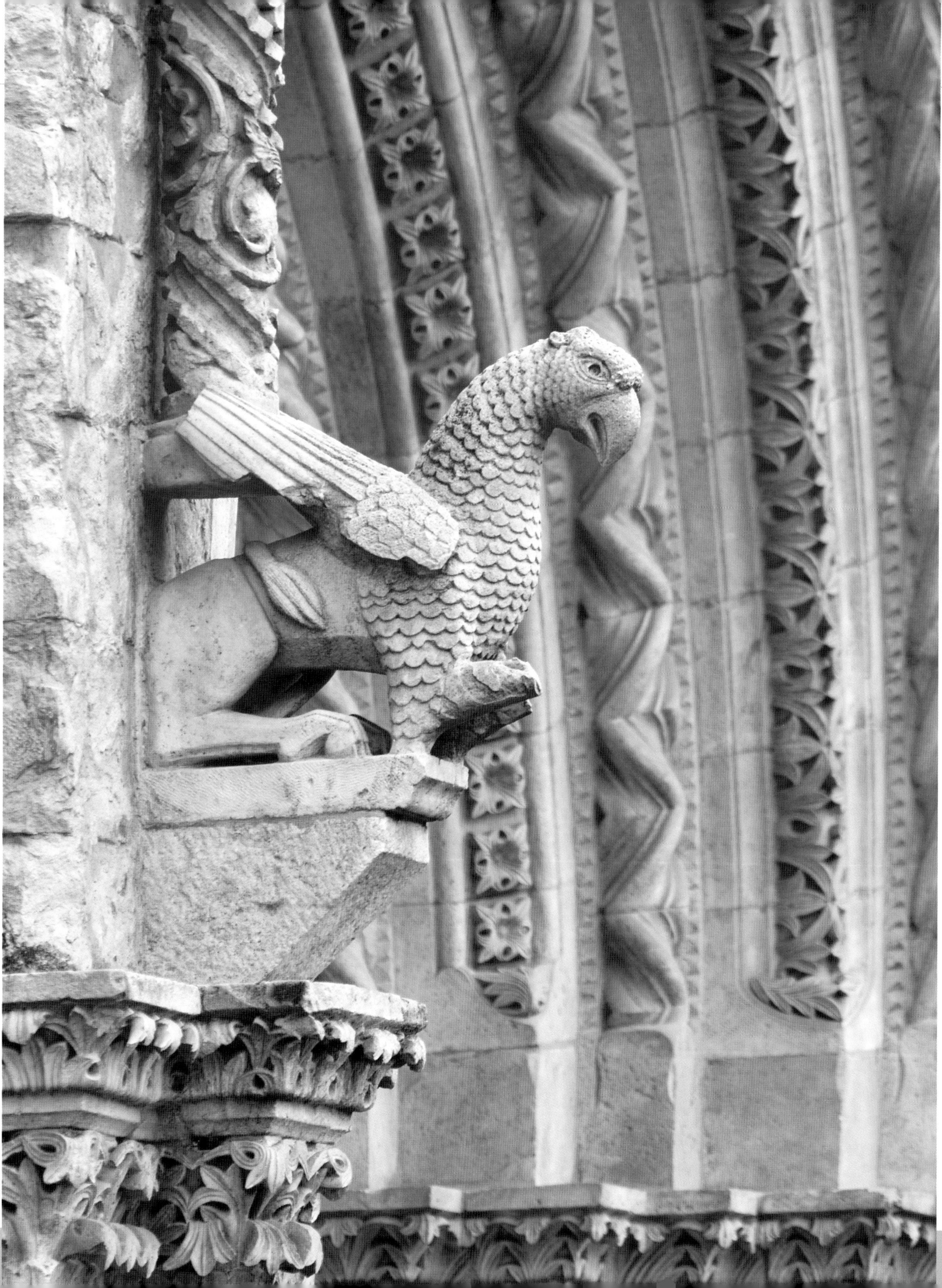

Cathedral carvings

LARINO, MOLISE

Built in the tenth and eleventh centuries and inaugurated in 1319, the Duomo dedicated to San Pardo of the small town of Larino, near Campobasso, is considered by many to be one of the finest examples of Gothic architecture in Italy. Its unusually sophisticated structure and delicate carvings may owe something to the fact that it was largely built by architects and engineers brought in from the French court. Larino, an important town since Roman times, also boasts an amphitheatre dating back to the first century AD.

Pizzeria

NAPLES, CAMPANIA

Pizza, the world's favourite food, is said by some to have been invented in the bustling metropolis of Naples, when the locals began to add tomato to their yeast-based flat bread. Hugging the coastline of the spectacular Bay of Naples, with the brooding volcano Vesuvius on the skyline to the south, Naples is a noisy, chaotic city. Capital of the *Mezzogiorno*, the land of the midday sun, it has gained a reputation as the bad boy of Italy, a city of danger and organized crime, but it is also a city that exudes excitement and unpredictability.

San Francesco di Paola

NAPLES, CAMPANIA

Modelled on Rome's Pantheon, the Neoclassical San Francesco di Paola was originally planned as a colonnaded building by King Joachim Murat (1767–1815) as a tribute to his brother-in-law, Emperor Napoleon (1769–1821). When King Ferdinand I (1503–64) was restored to the throne of Naples in 1816, he continued the work, converting the building to a church and completing it around 30 years later. A large, imposing dome, 53 metres (174 feet) high – 10 metres (33 feet) higher than its Roman cousin – presides over an impressive portico supported by six Ionic columns and two Ionic pillars.

Via San Gregorio Armeno

NAPLES, CAMPANIA

It is Christmas all year round in this extraordinary, narrow Neapolitan street, which is the centre for the crafting of the *presepe*, or nativity scene. At Christmas in Italy every village has its *presepe*, some unassuming, beautiful scenes at the roadside, others sophisticated Christmas theme parks where you pay admission and wander through the Christmas story. Entire nativity scenes or the figurines, buildings and other materials to make your own can be purchased here. In the *Museo Nazionale di San Martino* in Naples is the biggest *presepe* ever, the Presepe Cuciniello.

Looking towards Campanile

AMALFI, CAMPANIA

The southern side of the rocky peninsula south of Naples that reaches out into the Tyrrhenian Sea towards Cápri is the beautiful Amalfi Coast. It is dotted with picturesque fishing villages stacked above the sea, amongst which are enticing places such as Positano and Praiano, clinging precariously to steep cliffs. The views are breathtaking here, as are the restaurants selling freshly caught grilled fish, which can be washed down with the crisp, dry white wine, Lacrima Christi, grown on the slopes of Mount Vesuvius. Amalfi, the coast's largest town, was once an important sea-faring power.

View from Villa Rufolo Garden

AMALFI, CAMPANIA

The group of buildings, Arabic in style, that make up the Villa Rufolo were constructed in the 1270s by the noble Rufolo family as a symbol of their great wealth and prestige. The house is built around a courtyard surrounded by a beautifully ornate Moorish loggia. Neglected for several hundred years, the house and its exotic garden were restored in the mid-1800s by Scottish botanist Francis Neville Reid, just in time for the great German composer Richard Wagner (1813–83) to use it as the inspiration for his opera *Parsifal*.

Parco Archeologico

BAÍA, CAMPANIA

Baía was the holiday resort of hedonistic noble Romans who went there to enjoy its numerous thermal baths filled with warm mineral water that originated in sulphur springs below. Julius Caesar (100–44 BC) and Nero (AD 37–68) had villas there and they undoubtedly enjoyed the pleasures to be had at the town's domed casino. Although most of this ancient holiday region is now under water, the ruins to be explored in this superb archaeological park take us on a journey back in time, enabling us to imagine wealthy and powerful Romans at play.

Villa ruins

POMPEII, CAMPANIA

The catastrophe that struck the Roman town of Pompeii in AD 79 can only be imagined. There had been an earthquake 17 years previously but that served only as a prelude to the horror that must have been experienced on that August day when Mount Vesuvius finally erupted, spewing pumice and ash on to the town, destroying buildings and killing many of its inhabitants. Numerous Pompeiian household items were preserved as were the remains of the inhabitants, caught at the moment of their deaths and their outlines eerily, but beautifully preserved in plaster.

Lemon Grove

SORRENTO, CAMPANIA

Lemon groves, a small beach and relaxing cafés, nothing could be more different from the manic bustle of Naples or the baking ruins of Pompeii. Founded by the Greeks, Sorrento has been a destination for sun-worshippers since Roman times, a town of poetry and legend. Even its original name, *Surrentum*, has its origin in folklore, being linked to the legend of the Sirens. From its limestone bastion, you can look down upon the blue waters of the Gulf of Naples, sipping a cool limoncello, the delicious liqueur made from Sorrento lemons.

Piazza Umberto I

CÁPRI, CAMPANIA

Known familiarly since the 1930s as the 'Piazetta', the cramped Piazza Umberto I is the centre of the island of Cápri, a meeting place for tourists and locals alike. Located under a clock tower, this busy square is crowded with swish cafés where a coffee costs a king's ransom, but it is worth it to watch the well-dressed passers-by and hopefully for them to watch you! Cápri is, without question, the most beautiful of the three islands situated just outside the Gulf of Naples.

Rock window

VIESTE, PUGLIA

With its white limestone cliffs, grottoes, secluded beaches, sandy coves and ancient forests, the Gargano Peninsula is one of southern Italy's most beautiful areas. The views of the Adriatic's emerald-green waters are breathtaking and it is no wonder that sun-worshippers are drawn to its beautiful seaside towns such as Manfredonia, Peschici and the lovely whitewashed resort of Vieste. The beaches are spectacular. The Spiaggia del Castello for example is set against the backdrop of steep white cliffs, the dazzling white rocky monolith of Scoglio di Pozzomunno towering over it.

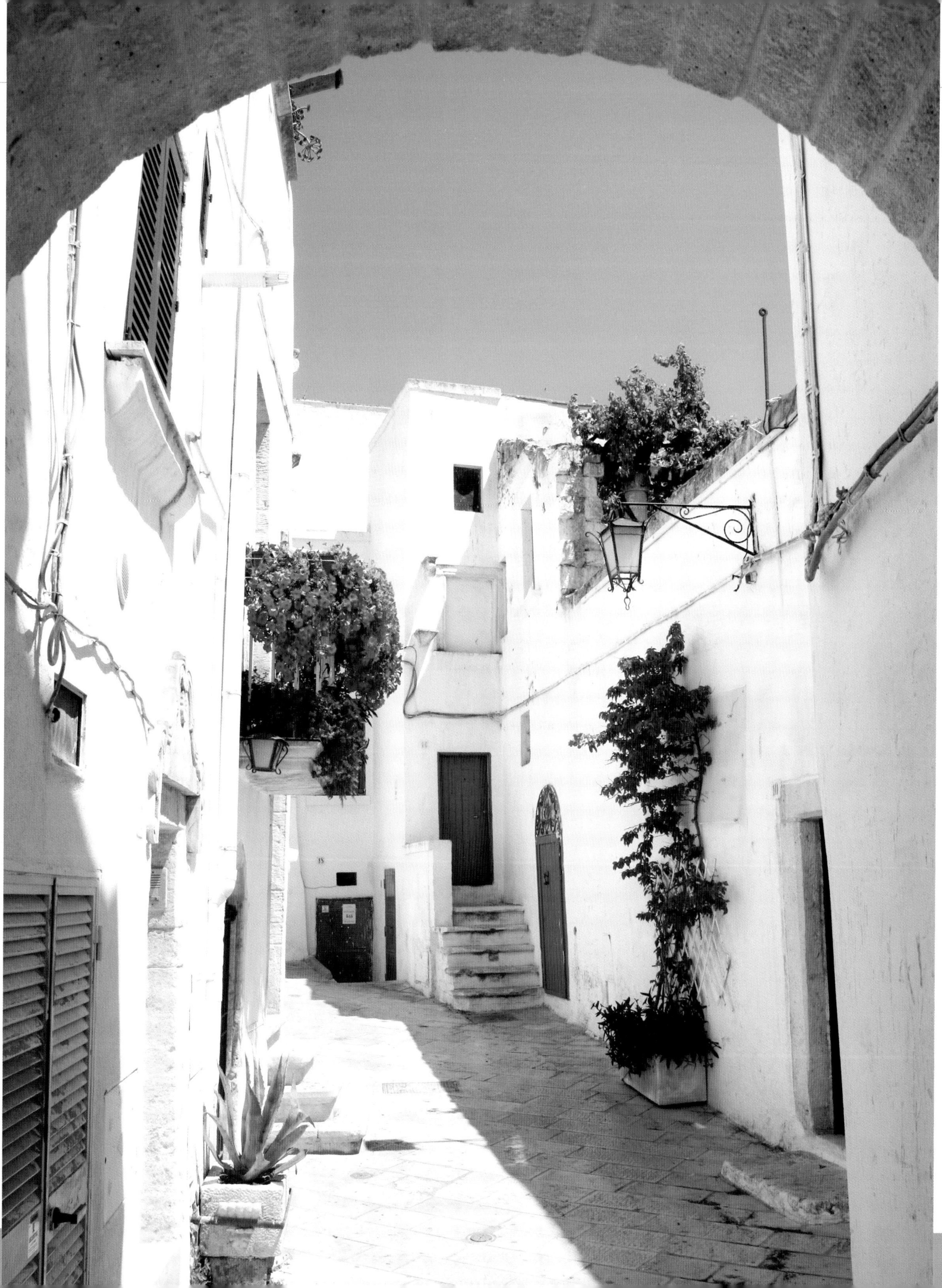

Courtyard

OSTUNI, PUGLIA

The deep blue of the Mediterranean sky contrasts stunningly with the charming whitewashed walls of the houses of this incomparably beautiful Puglian city. Known for obvious reasons as the 'White City', Ostuni is built on a series of levels, with narrow streets, stairways, arches and alleyways seeming to lead nowhere. It is situated on a hillside overlooking the coastal plain and has lovingly preserved its striking historical centre. Olive groves and vineyards abound around this paradise close to which lie a series of dazzling, unspoilt beaches.

Port

MOLFETTA, PUGLIA

The origins of the town of Molfetta on Italy's Adriatic coast are uncertain, although the remains of a Neolithic settlement have been uncovered. In 1522, it was given by Emperor Charles V (1500–58) to the Duke of Termoli, but was later sacked by the French. In 1631 Cesare II Gonzaga (1592–1632) included Molfetta in his princely titles, but the town changed ownership again nine years later when the Spinola family bought the fief. In 1798 it was incorporated into the royal domain. Molfetta has a lovely walled medieval town and a splendid Romanesque cathedral.

Trulli Houses

ALBEROBELLO, PUGLIA

The surreal, white, cone-topped dwellings known as *trulli* that line the narrow streets of the town of Alberobello have obscure origins, but may well have been a classic Italian tax dodge – the *trulli* could be easily dismantled when the tax collector arrived. They are circular, with extremely thick walls and conical roofs, which have a spire and are often decorated with symbols of religious or superstitious significance. Whitewashed on the outside, they fit in perfectly with the parched landscape of the area with its picturesque vineyards and olive groves.

Santa Croce Basilica

LECCE, PUGLIA

Cherubs abound in Lecce, the city situated on the heel of Italy and sometimes described as the 'Baroque Florence'. There are Roman ruins there but it was the seventeenth century that brought fame and prosperity to the area. Soon grandiose churches and palaces were appearing, built in the new *barocco Leccese* style and the soft stone of the area, *pietro di Lecce*, allowed artists to run riot with carvings of cherubs and other delightful decorative features as in the Basilica of Santa Croce with its richly ornate façade.

Maratea

TYRRHENIAN COAST, BASILICATA

Maratea is perhaps Italy's best-kept secret. Several hours south of Naples, on the Gulf of Policastro, it is situated on the slopes of Monte San Biagio on a stretch of the dramatic Basilicata coastline. Unspoilt and far more affordable than the Amalfi coast 160 kilometres (100 miles) to the north, the small port of Maratea consists of Maratea Inferiore, the small port, and Maratea Superiore, the old centre, which perches precariously on the ridges of two hills, one of which boasts a huge statue of Christ with arms extended.

Church of San Pietro Barisano and Sassi

MATERA, BASILICATA

Once occupied by Byzantine monks and then, from the fifteenth century, by local peasants, the extraordinary, limestone patchwork of cave-dwellings at Matera is one of the oldest and oddest towns in the world. Over time some of the *sassi*, as these grottoes are known, became quite grand and churches, such as San Pietro Barisano, were given elaborate façades. The poverty of the inhabitants led to them being re-housed in the 1950s, leaving us to marvel at the astonishing ingenuity of the people of Matera.

Castle

MELFI, BASILICATA

The magnificent Norman stronghold at Melfi broods over the buildings below, signifying the former importance of this medieval town. The Normans conquered this part of Italy in the eleventh century, making Melfi their capital and, indeed, it was at the castle that Pope Nicholas II (c. 990–1061) invested Norman leader Robert Guiscard (1015–85) with the duchies of Apulia, Calabria and Sicily in 1059. The castle now houses the Museo Nazinale del Melfese, with its wonderful collection of Byzantine jewellery.

Mural

DIAMANTE, CALABRIA

The sun shines all year round in Calabria, where the charming historic fishing village of Diamante with its array of beautiful beaches is situated. Nestled on a rock above the Mediterranean in order to protect it from flooding and the pirates who used to pillage this coast, Diamante became a canvas for poor painters of the early 1900s. Unable to afford their own materials, they expressed themselves in murals on the walls of the centuries-old stucco houses of the village, turning it into an extraordinary and unique art gallery.

Raganello Gorges

PARCO NAZIONALE POLLINO, CALABRIA

For 32 kilometres (20 miles) the spectacular 700-metre-deep (2,300 feet) Raganello Gorges cut through the Parco Nazionale Pollino, Italy's largest national park. Stretching through Basilicata and Calabria, Pollino, more than 1,800 square kilometres (695 square miles) in size, features both natural and archaeological points of interest. Golden eagles soar above Italy's last habitat for the rare Bosnian pine, symbol of the park. There are glacial cirques, large beech-tree woods, gorges and caves, as well as archaeological sites that date back to Greek colonization.

Santa Maria dell'Isola

TROPEA, CALABRIA

The buildings of Tropea, the prettiest town on Calabria's Tyrrhenian coast, seem to grow out of the cliffside on which they are perched, high above one of the town's superb beaches and the turquoise waters of the Mediterranean. Its unspoilt narrow, steep streets and centuries-old churches make it one of Calabria's most popular destinations. Facing the town is the large rock, once an island, at the top of which stands the former Benedictine sanctuary of Santa Maria della'Isola. Built in the Middle Ages, it looks disapprovingly down on the frolicking sun-worshippers below.

Fishing Boats

SOVERATO, CALABRIA

'The gem of the Ionian Sea' lazes in the sun at the southern tip of the Gulf of Squillace. The small town of Soverato gently bakes through the summer as visitors take to the beaches to bronze their bodies. But there are other things to do in Soverato besides sunbathing. The botanical garden contains an amazing variety of local plants and fauna; the sixteenth-century *Pietà A Gagini*, a fine example of Renaissance sculpture, is worth seeing as is the eighteenth-century Duomo. However, it is long hours on splendid sandy beaches that define this beautiful place.

Le Castella

ISOLA CAPO RIZZUTO, CALABRIA

The small town of Isola Capo Rizzuto is not actually an island. It stretches on an isthmus into the sea, at the northern end of the Gulf of Squillace, dominated by Le Castella, an imposing fortress that seems to rise magically out of the sea like a sandcastle that has been swamped by the tide. The fortification's origins may stretch back as far as the Second Punic War (218–201 BC) but it took its current form around 1521 just 15 years before it was plundered by Algerian pirate Khai-ad-din, known as 'Redbeard'.

Islands

THE RUGGED ISLAND OF SICILY IS THE LARGEST ISLAND IN THE MEDITERRANEAN, SITUATED AT THE HISTORIC CROSSROADS OF THE TRADE ROUTES THAT USED TO PLY THAT SEA. IT HAS ALSO BEEN MUCH CONQUERED LEADING TO ITS BEING DESCRIBED AS THE WORLD'S FIRST MULTICULTURAL SOCIETY, HAVING BEEN IN ITS TIME A GREEK COLONY, A ROMAN PROVINCE, AN ARAB EMIRATE, A NORMAN KINGDOM AND THEN AN ARAGONESE ONE.

It is an eclectic place, a European island, but one with strong African and Asian influences; a place that has been fashioned by a history that has left a fascinating legacy of Punic cities, Greek temples, Roman ruins, Norman castles and Aragonese churches. It is also home to heavenly beaches and incomparable scenic beauty.

Many ponder the question of whether this island can actually be considered Italian. After all, they argue, there is probably more Greek, Arabic, Phoenician, Spanish and Norman blood flowing in Sicilian veins than Italian. But that is not really the point. It is just this collision of cultures that makes Sicily the fascinating enigma that it is.

The other great Italian island of the Mediterranean, Sardinia, is very different to Sicily. Whereas Sicily has been borne on the waves of history, Sardinia has been, as D.H. Lawrence (1885–1930) once wrote, 'left outside of time and history'. Its ancient history endures in the shape of the mysterious *nuraghe,* but the island is now a fabulous playground with extraordinary beaches and, sometimes, extraordinary prices.

Valle dei Templi

AGRIGENTO, SICILY

The magnificent Temple of Concord sits majestically atop a rocky escarpment south of the town of Agrigento. Following its founding as a Greek colony in the sixth century BC, Agrigento became one of the leading Mediterranean cities, its prestige and prosperity evident in the astonishing collection of Doric temples that look down on the ancient town, several of which are more or less intact. Through the centuries these echoes of a lost age have provided inspiration for artists, writers and poets.

Botanical Garden

PALERMO, SICILY

The largest of Italy's wonderful botanical gardens, the one at Palermo dates back to 1779, when the Royal Academy of Studies established a botanical institute in the city. Nowadays it provides something of an oasis in the middle of this bustling Sicilian city, housing an impressive array of tropical and semi-tropical plants, both native and foreign. Indeed, many of these plants were first introduced into Europe by these gardens, which moved to their present site adjacent to the Villa Giulia Park in 1786. Neoclassical structures were later added to its attractions.

Cattedrale

PALERMO, SICILY

The architectural chaos of the imposing Cathedral of Santa Maria Assunta seems to match the noisy chaos of the city in which it is situated. The conquering Normans, who ruled much of southern Italy at the time, built the church in 1185 on the site of a mosque, which in turn had replaced an earlier Christian basilica. Gothic elements were added in the thirteenth and fourteenth centuries and the Spaniards added to it in the fifteenth. Finally, the late eighteenth and early nineteenth centuries introduced ornate Neoclassical touches.

Mercato del Capo

PALERMO, SICILY

Palermo's markets have echoes of the Arabic culture that dominated the region 1,000 years ago. Indeed, as you push between the colourful stalls, you would be forgiven for thinking you were in North Africa. Situated in the ancient streets of Via Volturno, Via Beati Paoli and Via Porta Carini in Mercato del Capo, the city's second biggest market, you can buy just about anything, including the local delicacies of *purpu* (boiled octopus), *pahelle* (pan-cakes made of peas), fresh artichokes and fruits marinated in wine.

Duomo mosaics

MONREALE, SICILY

The glorious golden mosaics of the Duomo at Monreale are a reminder of the wealth and power of the Normans in the twelfth century. Completed in 1182 by Byzantine and Sicilian artists, they depict scenes from the Old Testament in the nave, the teachings of Christ in the aisles, choir and transepts, and the Gospels in the side apses. The intricate column decoration and the magnificent bronze doors of the cloisters are exceptional, but there is much more to admire in this architectural masterpiece founded by Norman King William II in 1172.

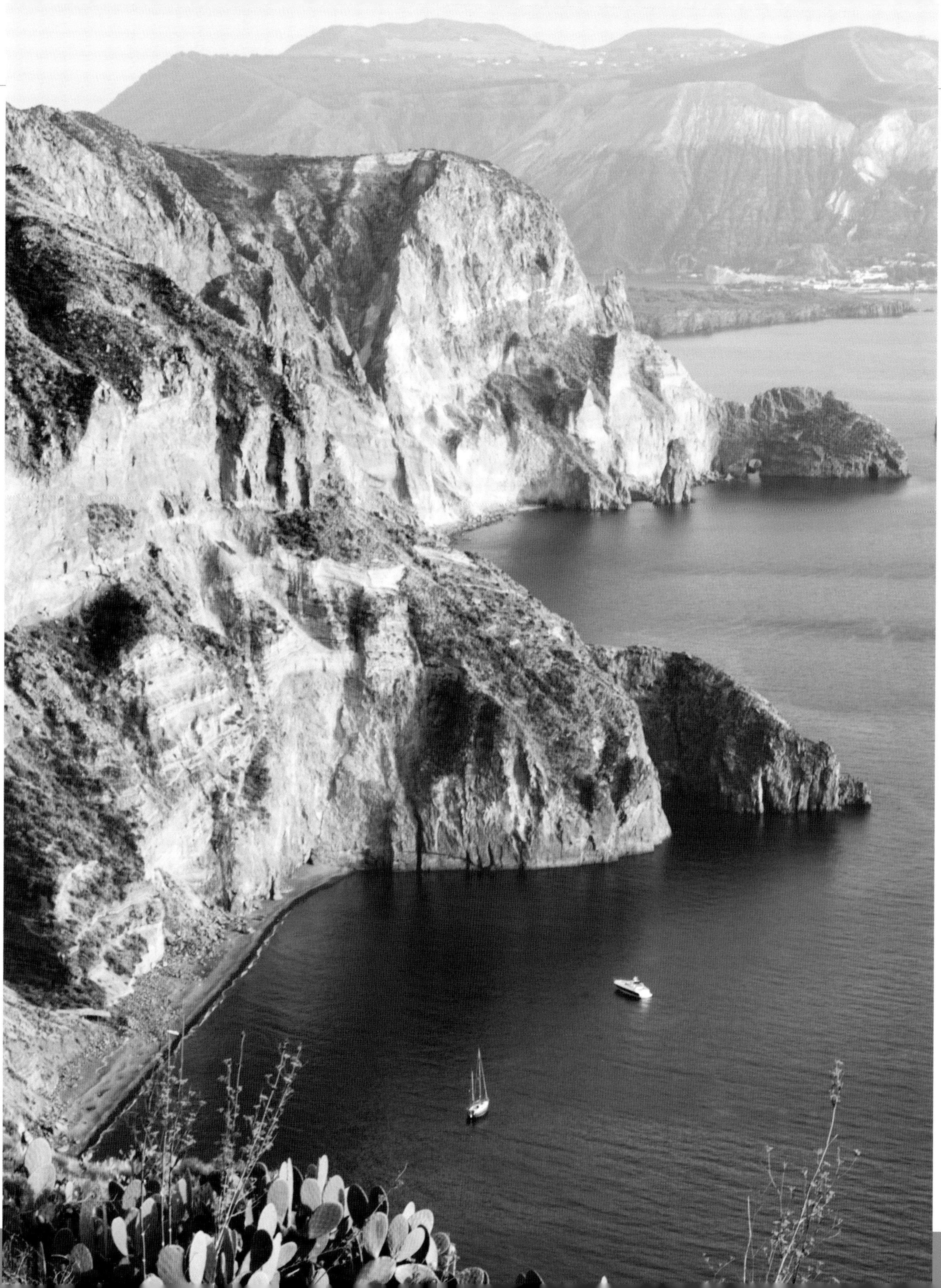

Looking towards Lípari

AEOLIAN ISLANDS, SICILY

The god of the winds, Aeolus, presides over the volcanic archipelago of the Aeolian Islands, stretching across the gap between the volcanoes Etna and Vesuvius in the Tyrrhenian Sea just off the coast of Sicily. Renowned for its perfect climate and its chain of active volcanoes, its main islands of Lípari, Salina, Filicudi, Alicudi, Stromboli, Panarea and Vulcano are rugged with steep cliffs, deep caverns and magnificent views. The largest, Lípari, is famous for its fabulous beaches as well as its pumice stone that is shipped all over the world.

Teatro Greco

TAORMINA, SICILY

Mount Etna broods in the far distance, a spectacular sight viewed from the seats of the Teatro Greco in Taormina. Built by the Greeks in the third century BC, the theatre was later re-built by the Romans. But Taormina, capital of Byzantine Sicily in the ninth century, offers the chance to visit many other Classical remains. The town itself, with its thirteenth-century fortress-like Duomo, is an almost perfectly preserved medieval town, but is also Sicily's most glamorous resort, the haunt in the past of writers, artists, aristocrats and royals.

Mount Etna

NEAR CATANIA, SICILY

Described by the Romans as the forge of Vulcan, god of fire, at 3,370 metres (11,056 feet) Mount Etna is Europe's highest volcano. It is also the liveliest, having erupted at least five times in the twenty-first century. However, even as its activity continues, this spectacular mountain also offers skiing in winter months and in the summer hikers can enjoy the spectacular walks in the woods that cover the mountain. There is a wide variety of wildlife and occasionally a golden eagle might be seen riding the thermals high above you.

Duomo

SIRACUSA, SICILY

The rich Greek history of the 2,700-year-old city of Siracusa can be read in the architecture of its extraordinary seventh-century Duomo. The massive Doric columns of the Greek Temple of Athena that previously occupied the site are still visible, though shaken by earthquakes over the centuries. Above the columns other elements of Siracusa's past can be seen in its Norman nave, while the façade is a Baroque replacement following the damage done to the previous one by the powerful earthquake of 1693.

Cave dwellings

FAVIGNANA, SICILY

The ruggedly beautiful and small island of Favignana, the largest of the three principal Egadi Islands, sits seven kilometres (4.4 miles) west of the coast of Sicily. It is an island famous for its caves, cut out of sandstone rock, which served as dwellings at the dawn of mankind. Today, its crystal-clear water makes it a paradise for divers and snorkellers, who can explore spectacular underwater sights. Favignana is one of the few places on earth where the Arabian fishing technique of *tonnara* is still used for the trapping and *mattanza* (killing) of bluefin tuna.

Piazza Municipio

NOTO, SICILY

Following the catastrophic earthquake of 1693 many Sicilian towns and villages were re-constructed in the style of the time – Baroque. The pleasant little town of Noto was re-built from scratch, designed for functionality and the architectural harmony for which the Baroque strived. Today, you will find in its centre elegantly crumbling Baroque palazzi, churches and houses with elaborate façades and delicately ornate balconies. Meanwhile, the Piazza Municipio provides a fine point from which to view the descendants of those lovers of the Baroque making their *passeggiata* after church on a Sunday morning.

Street scene

CÁGLIARI, SARDINIA

D.H. Lawrence described the ancient port city of Cágliari as 'strange and rather wonderful, not a bit like Italy'. It straddles a long bay between the sparkling blue water of the Golfo di Cágliari and the burnt ochre fields inland. In truth, little has changed since Lawrence made his observation in 1921. In Cágliari's medieval quarter the Castello perches on a hill, guarded by a limestone wall and towers constructed in the fourteenth century. There are fourteenth- and fifteenth-century palazzi and churches and dimly lit bars and restaurants in which to while away the evenings.

Basilica di San Saturno

CÁGLIARI, SARDINIA

Dedicated to Saturninus of Cágliari, the patron saint of Cágliari, who was martyred during the reign of Roman Emperor Diocletian (AD 244–311), the fifth-century Basilica of San Saturno is one of the most important and most ancient in Sardinia. Parts of the original structure – the central part and the dome – remain, to which extensions have been added, one of which includes a nave and two aisles.

Ruins

THARROS, SARDINIA

A visit to the ruins of the ancient city of Tharros is a visit into the past, a past that includes its founding by Phoenicians and its habitation by Punics followed by Romans. In the tenth century it was finally abandoned in the face of constant incursions by Saracens from the east, and from that time onwards, sadly, the site served as a quarry for building materials for the surrounding towns and villages. The ruins in this fascinating open-air museum featuring baths, temples, houses and workshops are mainly Roman and early Christian.

Fishing Boats

BOSA, SARDINIA

The picturesque little town of Bosa is located at the mouth of the Temo River in the Planargia flatlands on Sardinia's north-west coast. The buildings of its ancient Sa Costa quarter clamber up a low hill topped by the sturdy Castello di Serravalle, built for the Malaspina family in the twelfth century. Its narrow streets and alleyways, where tourists are relatively rare, are little changed since the Middle Ages. By the river stand the fifteenth-century Aragonese-Gothic Duomo and the eleventh-century Romanesque San Pietro Extramuros.

Dome of San Michele Church

ALGHERO, SARDINIA

Although it sits on the west coast of Sardinia on a peninsula facing the Bay of Alghero, the lovely town of Alghero is not really Sardinian. Founded by Arabs and ruled by the Genoese in the Middle Ages, in 1355 it fell under Spanish control when the Aragonese seized it in the name of the pope. Today it retains a distinctly Catalan feel, which can be seen in the Catalan-Gothic of its Cattedrale di Santa Maria Immacolata di Alghero, as demonstrated by its beautifully colourful dome.

Coloured pasta

VILLASIMIUS, SARDINIA

Sardinian cuisine is inextricably linked to the production of wheat and flour and in fact the Romans called the island 'the granary of Rome'. The dried pastas that we cook today almost certainly originated on Sardinia, where the locals have always left their pasta to dry in the sun. Nowadays, it is mostly tourists who can be seen lying in the sun, and at the small town of Villasimius east of Cágliari on the island's south-eastern corner they are afforded ample opportunity by long, inviting stretches of sandy beach and secluded coves.

Stella Maris Church

COSTA SMERALDA, SARDINIA

Between the gulfs of Cugnana and Arzachena lies the Costa Smeralda, the playground of the beautiful people and the super-rich who fly into the island on their private jets or sail into the marina at Porto Cervo on board their huge yachts. Supposedly founded by a fabulously wealthy consortium in the 1950s, Costa Smeralda has numerous sequestered beaches with fabulous views. A masterpiece of modern church architecture, the beautiful Stella Maris Church overlooks Porto Cervo's old port, an intense painting by El Greco (1541–1614) in one of its niches.

Su Nuraxi Nuraghe

NEAR BARTÚMINI, SARDINIA

The people who built the 7,000 or so *nuraghe* on the island of Sardinia remain unknown to this day. They left no written word and all we can surmise is that they were well organized and, from the evidence of these remarkable conical basalt block structures, possessed extraordinary engineering skills. Situated on a small plateau, the impregnable fortified complex of the Su Nuraxi Nuraghe, dating back to 1478 BC, is one of an estimated 30,000 that were originally built by this enigmatic people.

La Spiaggia della Pelosa

NEAR STINTINO, SARDINIA

The impossibly crystal-clear, azure waters of the Spiaggia della Pelosa are what attract people to the beautiful peninsular resort of Stintino at the western end of the Golfo dell'Asinara on the north Sardinian coast. Until fairly recently Stintino was little more than a collection of ramshackle fishermen's cottages situated between two harbours, but even though it has now been well and truly discovered by tourists, this rugged and spectacular corner of Sardinia remains a quiet, laid-back and as yet fairly unspoilt place.

Index

Page numbers in *italics* indicate illustrations.